Lung

Young British Poets for Oxfam

edited by

dd Swift & Kim Lockwood

ith a preamble by David Lehman

INDEPENDENT INNOVATIVE INTERNATIONAL

EYEWEAR PUBLISHING

Published by Cinnamon Press
Meirion House, Glan yr afon, Tanygrisiau
Blaenau Ffestiniog, Gwynedd, LL41 3SU
www.cinnamonpress.com
in collaboration with Eyewear Publishing

The right of the contributors to be identified as the authors of this work
has been asserted by them in accordance with the Copyright, Designs and
Patent Act, 1988. Copyright © 2012
ISBN: 978-1-907090-62-2
British Library Cataloguing in Publication Data. A CIP record for this
book can be obtained from the British Library.

Designed and typeset in Palatino by Cinnamon Press.
Cover from original artwork, 'Reflection of Birmingham's Eye' by
Jonathan Lewis © agency dreamstime Cover design by Jan Fortune
Printed in Poland
Cinnamon Press is represented in the UK by Inpress Ltd
www.inpressbooks.co.uk and in Wales by the Welsh Books Council
www.cllc.org.uk.

Special thanks to Kingston University Writing School for their generous
support of this book.

KINGSTON **WRITING SCHOOL**

All profits from this publication will go to assist the work of Oxfam.

Oxfam

Acknowledgments

The editors wish to thank the following – Kim Lockwood, her parents. Todd
Swift – his wife. Thanks to Martin Penny at Oxfam Books & Music,
Marylebone, for his on-going support of British poetry. Thanks to Oxfam for

their support of this project, Dr Jan Fortune for taking this big book on, Dr David Rogers at Kingston University for his support of creative writers, and Eyewear Publishing and its sponsors. A special thank you to Beverley Nadin, for letting us use the title of one of her poems for the title of this collection.

All reasonable efforts have been made to trace permissions and any missing will be gladly added at a later printing. All poems remain the copyright of the poets, who have kindly waived their rights for the purposes of this collection, as a donation for Oxfam. The editors thank them for their generosity. A few poems have appeared in previous publications and appear here with kind permission of the publisher, as arranged by the poets.

'The Centre', from *The Snowboy* by Mark Burnhope (Salt, 2011). 'Seasons in the Frame Shop', from *Antler* by John Clegg (Salt, 2012). 'Zelda in the Asylum', from *The Book I Never Wrote* by Ross Cogan (Overstope, 2012). 'Breaking Horses', from *Other Beasts* by Sarah Corbett (Seren, 2008). 'To his Uncool Mistress [after Marvell]', from *Selected: Love / All That / & OK* by Emily Critchley (Penned in the Margins, 2011). 'Tall Glass', from *Caribou* by Amy De'Ath' (Bad Press, 2011). All My Friends Regardless', from *Faber New Poets 5* by Joe Dunthorne (Faber & Faber, 2010). 'Hunch', from *Clueless Dogs* by Rhian Edwards (Seren, 2012). 'The Debt Collector' from *Here Comes The Night* by Alan Gillis (Gallery Press, 2010). 'Prenatal Polar Bear', from *Nigh-No-Place* by Jen Hadfield (Bloodaxe, 2008). 'Cutting A Figure' from *Beloved, in case you've been wondering* by Wayne Holloway-Smith (Donut Press, 2011). 'Listening to Kings of Convenience', from *The Bus from Belfast* by Andrew Jamison (Templar, 2011). 'Home', from *A Kind of Awe* by Joshua Jones (Red Ceilings, 2011). 'Iarlles y Ffynawn', from *Regeneration* by Meirion Jordan (Seren, 2012). 'Interiorana', from *Instead of Stars* by Amy Key (Tall-Lighthouse). 'Kolya's Nails' from *One Eye'd Leigh* by Katharine Kilalea (Carcanet, 2009). 'The Magnolia', from *The Magnolia* by Richard Lambert (Rialto, 2008). 'November Meals on Wheels', from *Budapest To Babel* by Agnes Lehoczky (Eggbox, 2008). 'Fist', from *The Hitcher* by Hannah Lowe (Rialto, 2011). 'Spinning Plates' from *The 2012 Collection* by Richie McCaffrey (HappenStance). 'June 16, 1956. The Church of St. George', from *The Marble Orchard* by Sandeep Parmar (Shearsman, 2012). 'Un-History' from *Pure Hustle* by Kate Potts (Bloodaxe, 2011). 'Rapture' from *Breaking Silence* by Jacob Sam-La Rose (Bloodaxe, 2011). 'Rusty Sea' from *Low-tide Lottery* by Claire Trévien (Salt, 2011). 'Μνημοσύνη', from *Confer* by Ahren Warner (Bloodaxe, 2011). 'Slide Rule', from *Electric Shadow* by Heidi Williamson (Bloodaxe, 2011). 'Iconostasis', from *Initiate: An Oxford Anthology of New Writing* by Alice Willington (Blackwell, 2010). 'Loughborough', from *High Performance* by Luke Wright (Nasty Little Press, 2009).

Preamble to the New British Poetry

The new British poetry, as represented in this volume, is – to borrow from the poems – 'buxom, brazen' (Tiffany Anne Tondut) and 'jazzed up' (Simon Turner). It can be 'deft and elegant' (Joanne Limburg), 'buttoned-down / in tweed and scarved' on the Mersey (Evan Jones) but is more likely to arrive 'unshaven and barefoot, as if on a pilgrimage' (André Naffis-Sahley). It spends time 'in downtown dives' (Anna Johnson), on 'nuclear nights in London' and other cities (Siddhartha Bose), 'at those dangerous margins / of sleep where anything can be true' (Alexander Freer), raging 'against this priggish darkness' (Melanie Challenger).

The poets worry that 'we'll never find a common tongue' (Anne Welsh); they have been 'applauded for [their] no-nonsense take on the infantilism of [their] generation' (Luke Kennard); they lust for 'the vague, ecstatic kisses / Of a mad mind flushed to profligate invention' (Abigail Parry). The objects of their contemplation include the 'odd regatta' of coloured hosiery in the spun cycle (Heather Phillipson), the resemblance between a French kiss and the taking of communion (Lorraine Mariner), and the mysterious 'third person standing at the foot of the bed, / watching us sleep' and inspiring the poet to undertake a villanelle (Sophie Mackintosh).

Not long ago the line of the English poetic tradition was narrowly defined. You would regularly encounter poems too saturated in their antecedents: poems about the class struggle, bad lovemaking with a carbuncular person, the need to have a piss in the middle of the night, chance meetings on rural roads with decrepit old men who display impressively sturdy minds.

The influences on the new British poets are as varied as globalisation and wide demographics allow. You still get your Eliot and your Marvell. In Emily Critchley's clever take on 'To His Coy Mistress' she switches gender identities on us: 'were I a man, / For whom love studied & love unattained / Were less vivid, resounded less than the *real thing*; / I'd sit & think & walk & pass my days / With you in true mutual bliss.' There are further twists: the poet complains that Marvell's 'amorous bird of prey' has turned acquiescent, 'the tamed grown tamer,' and so self-pleasure appears to be the speaker's preferred option.

You get your dose of T. S. Eliot in Caleb Klaces's 'Plastic holy,' which begins with a child's untutored image of 'the Berlin Wall' ('as thick as my house / and hollowed out like a baguette') and ends with an ironic echo of the 'Marie' lines in the first stanza of 'The Waste Land.'

But the poets also give you Cavafy, a named influence in two of the poems, and they assimilate Beckett, the art of translation, Elizabeth Bishop, Emily Dickinson, booze, Ecstasy, robotics, the ruins of Coventry, American dreams, British movies of the 1940s. They derive more of their energy from Louis Armstrong's Hot Five or the bluesy voice of Ray Charles than from Berlioz or Debussy, though the latter float in and are welcome when they do. Rhyme is scarce. The word *jazz* shows up here and there undefined and stripped of an immediate musical context – as in John Challis's 'Jazz Maggot' – as if the term itself constituted a kind of speakeasy code that will admit you to the club.

Simon Turner's 'Brummagern Jazz' sounds the book's keynote: 'What a feeling, to step out of the musty / twilight bookshop air with a collection / of poetry under your arm & run smack / into a bleach-blonde brassy bellow of a day.' Claire Askew lingers at the bookshop, generating metaphors from the physical objects we are in danger of losing in our electronic age. 'I like to bend them to my will – / turn their spines inverse like gymnasts,' Askew writes in 'Books.' The books wait for her 'on bookstore shelves, / asleep, stiff as exclamation marks – / and my fingers itch to break in every one.'

In 'Three Strikes,' Caroline Bird beguiles this Yank with her English intonation when she borrows the style of Gertrude Stein and applies it to America's national pastime: 'I lost one and then I lost the other. / I lost one to keep the other / but the other didn't want to be kept, / not like that, not as an accidental / second catch of the baseball match / with your palm outstretched to feel for rain.' Though I have followed baseball closely all my life, I do not know what 'an accidental / second catch' can possibly mean, but that is not to the detriment of the poem.

The subject of lust – as a deadly sin but an irresistible one – provokes Tiffany Anne Tondut's 'Way of a Wanton' with its tidy closing rhyme: 'I burn / for you, your / deadly wick. / You give me / fever, a rash / I want to lick.' Of the first lines in the book, the one that seems to be echoing the longest in my brain is Sophie Mayer's 'Today is the day of the smashing of dishes.' But I would close this preamble with my joy in Sophie Hannah's conjoining of the new and the old in a poem whose end words include 'litter,' 'Gary Glitter,' 'quitter,' and 'bitter': 'I am following the Dalai Lama on Twitter / But the Dalai Lama is not following me.'

David Lehman
New York, 28 Sept 2011

Introduction

Lung Jazz: Young British Poets for Oxfam is an extraordinary gathering of poems that define a generation. These poems have all been donated to Oxfam by the poets themselves, with, in some cases, the support of major publishers. As such, this book is a double pleasure – it makes a wonderful introduction to the poetry being written today in Britain, but it also manages to allow poetry to make something happen, by raising funds and awareness for an important charity. Since 2004, when I became Oxfam GB's Poet-in-residence, based in Martin Penny's Marylebone shop, poets have supported Oxfam brilliantly.

Our very first evening featured Sir Andrew Motion, Wendy Cope, Charlie Dark and Patience Agbabi – since then, over two-hundred of the major poets of the UK have read for this ongoing project, on DVDs, CDs, and in-shop. Tens of thousands of pounds have been raised by this project.

The selection process that the editors faced was challenging. We first made an open call for poets to send us their best new work; the only criteria were that the poets should consider themselves part of the British poetry community, and have been born in or after 1970. This way, we felt, we could capture the multicultural and international vibrancy of the poetry scene as it unfolds in the 21st century, and showcase the new sense of originality and energy that these Young British Poets (YBPs) represent.

We were soon inundated, with around 3000 poems, and it became clear that we would only be able to take a fraction of what had been sent our way; and only one poem per poet, at that. As important precursor books such as *The Salt Book of Younger Poets* and Bloodaxe's *Voice Recognition* have argued, this is evidently a poetic generation unlike any before.

Readers of this anthology are likely familiar with the leading names in British poetry, in the post-Larkin, post-Hughes generation, poets in their late 40s and older (Sir Geoffrey Hill, Denise Riley, Sir Andrew Motion, Wendy Cope, Simon Armitage, Carol Ann Duffy, Don Paterson, Alice Oswald, Paul Farley, Fiona Sampson, John Burnside, Jo Shapcott, Roddy Lumsden, to name a key few). To this list could be added the Irish giants, Muldoon and Heaney. However, below this impressive group is a momentous shift in poetic talent – and not only in terms of velocity and volume, though impressive these be

Due to a number of factors, not least new educational opportunities (creative writing courses), social networking, and pro-active Arts Council funding, poetry became a genre of viable interest to thousands of young British people in the 21st century. Poetry has always been popular, in some ways, with the young (one thinks of the 60s), but this time that interest has been backed up by a far more serious history of publications.

Reading over the many submitted poets, it was very difficult to find poorly-written poems. The general standard was high, provocatively so. Nor were the biographical sketches less than impressive. These are prize-winning, published, ambitious and well-educated young people, clearly inspired by the poetic traditions of the past, but with their own visions. This is as talented a generation as that of the Thirties or Fifties – perhaps the most talented since the Romantic era.

Some critics would argue that these high standards are a result of slick competence engineered by creative writing workshops; we have seen the impact of workshops as, rather, encouraging – greater reading, critical acumen, editing skills, and a sense of quality control. Poets are acting more 'professionally' sooner. This may, in the long run, spell the end of a bumbling amateurism beloved by some, but it is also a godsend for poetry lovers.

We selected poems that we felt would stand the test of time. Our reading of earlier generational anthologies suggested that, despite the melancholy fact of critical oblivion for most 'minor poets', a well-selected anthology piece can retain its interest for decades, if not centuries. As such, we had one eye on posterity. We asked ourselves, is this poem not just speaking to today, but to the eternal sense of poetic excellence that a meaningful canon can and still does represent?

Tested thus, the poems we wanted, and found, had to be original, formally skillful, and, in some way, thrilling. They had to stop us in our tracks as readers, and elicit the highest compliment one poet can pay to another: *I wish I'd written that.*

Obviously, the two editors did not agree on all submissions (and some favourites of one had to be excluded), but by seeking agreement, we have certainly compiled a far stronger roster. In a few cases we called newly-classic poems in, to tell the whole story; and, with a very few exceptions, feel that all the poets one needs to read to know this moment are, finally, included. Readers of *Lung Jazz* will not only discover poems of humour, exuberance, and conviction, but have an unparalleled opportunity to gain an instant overview of the poetic figures that will shape the next years and decades.

Todd Swift
London, 14 February 2012

Contents

Paul Adrian

Starlings

One wing jams, its faulty angle a hook
to drop one bird full pat into the sand.

The undulating shatter of the flock
continues, oblivious to its lost

equation. Two eyes out of a million
know the million's murmuration.

Rowyda Amin

Dear Ludovic

The wards are arranged according to the constellations, my bed in the upper pan of Libra. My elderly neighbour cat-sleeps to avoid the mother who hovers over his bed like marsh gas, moueing because he won't leave with her. There's little to admire through the window besides the garden and that is pocked by grave robbers rooting up nasturtiums in search of plastic bangles.

The small nurse with the Nefertiti eyes comes by every six clicks on the morphine drip, swinging a brain-hook with panache. She doesn't like my writing but never intervenes, more worried by the bird-headed man seen looking in through the third-floor windows of the cafeteria.

You should've been here for the masked ball in the pathology lab when the surgeons came as surgeons, the nurses as nurses and the pathologists, giggling, as a group of sanitation inspectors with laminated name tags. The test tube reliquaries gave a heart-warm glow when the minute came to give each other mouth-to-mouth. Ever since, they can't stop flirting. The locum overdosed me three times, licking her cherry vanilla lips at the ward sister.

Claire Askew

Books

I like to bend them to my will –
turn their spines inverse like gymnasts,
crack their skin 'til it's crazed and veined
like an old lady's palm. I deface the pages:
marginalia scattered and stark as a rash,
corners folded, fingered thin and soft
as a cotton fiver, circled
with the cold, grey footprints of tea.

I like them lived in as a marriage bed,
loose enough to open of their own accord
and shock me with a lucky-dip of verse.
The chatter-spit of ancient binding:
pages coming out in chunks like teeth.
They wait for me on bookstore shelves,
asleep, stiff as exclamation marks –
and my fingers itch to break in every one.

Tiffany Atkinson

First communion

The body of Christ
comes down in a flurry
of fresh white collectables.

It drifts in the palm like
a flake of soap or fish

yet has been known to burn
clean through the hand
and then the whole world.

Flat and tooled and matte
and odourless, what won't it
slip through: what does it *want*
that it travels such distances
pressed and papery with hurt?

Back in the clay it is anyone's.
Doesn't it run through the woods

after any old thing with one
hell of a din and no anorak,
hunting down heaven knows what?

Giuseppe Bartoli

The final glyph
*A glyph is a symbol (as a curved arrow on a road sign) that conveys
information nonverbally.*

I pause the song because /
I can't remember any more /

                       my father being handcuffed and
chained by multiple US government agents holding machine guns
instead of warrants at five o'clock in the morning / the taste of grade A
synthetic supermarket see-through squeeze bottle maple syrup in the
shape of a woman on sale in aisle two / how the Florida State Receiver
later instructed the armed mercenaries to rummage like rabid badgers
through the abode by leaving each room in the shape of an overturned
garbage can / the pain caused by autumnal crosswinds carving out
facial imperfections like a conduit or close where tears can stagnate /
my mother's hysteric bellows as she watched a bunch of unmasked
strangers break up twenty years of marriage floorboard by floorboard /
the sound of each snowflake committing hara-kiri is murder under the
weight of chained tires /

                       the song starts up
again /
         and it is I who breaks down and cries \

Jay Bernard

Lamplighters

The remaining stops
    are for the girl with
        languid children and the lanky

Eritrean with a blue plastic bag
    against his beige trousers.
        The classy ones got off.

Sucks for them!
        The best station looks
    out at the black universe
        whited-out with strip lights along

the concourse. They flicker like
    old fashioned lanterns I heard about
        lit by lamplighters who walked

from post to post across the city
    standing for a moment to torch
        the wick, then moving

through the intermittent dark through
    streets with no architecture
        just figures coming and going

like shy housemates in the kitchen.
    Sometimes I think I know
        the faces coming towards me

half shadow, half train-light distortion
    and we both avert our eyes
        in case of recognition

but I use the time when I know I am nothing
    but an awkward stranger to look up
        and stare them in the face.

Emily Berry

Devil Music

I bit on the absolute nerve.
It was a string that played me
into the desert. I used to wake
in the night with my saliva all dried up
and my stomach hollow as a dust bowl.
It was lonely as hell. I tapped my foot
but I didn't want to. I shut my mouth
in case the great chords rolled out
and they made a cigar-box guitar
out of me. It's your blues twang, they said.
It's your prayer. But I had no wish
to pray. To hell with this picking
and plucking that wrings a song from me.
That absolute nerve. The way it had me
by the tongue and the Achilles tendons,
oh, brother. I had to take charge of my life.
I bit down so it couldn't move or sing.
I put on my suit and tie. I had my first
barbershop shave and I scrubbed up
nice and clean. Let a man be a man,
I said to the mirror and saluted him,
cocking my hand like a pistol. I ground
my teeth to make the wheels turn
in my jaw. I worked. I silenced myself
devotedly until my devil soul twisted
and bucked, and was still.

Liz Berry

Horse

There was a horse inside her,
white and gymnastic as those
born kneeling in the fields that Spring.

Once she'd discovered it, she wanted nothing
but to ride, to slip the catch on the stable
and press her mouth to its mane,

tilting its nose to the sweetness
of hay and dusk air. She named it
but it bucked all words, answered only touch:

the beckoning of palm on a velvet ear,
the clamp of knee upon mud-specked flank.
Freed, it tossed any bridle but skin.

Old women tutted to see them jump,
feel the air stir. Her mother
whisked her legs with a slender crop

but at night it came, stamping her name
in the paddock of sheets,
rearing on elegant ankles in the coltsfoot.

She was bareback then, wild
in the frost, breath a snort, her heart
bolting for more in the dark.

Caroline Bird

Three Strikes

I lost one and then I lost the other.
I lost one to keep the other
but the other didn't want to be kept,
not like that, not as an accidental
second catch of the baseball match
with your palm outstretched to feel for rain.
The first didn't want to be lost
or kept, it was tricky. Dabbles of light
came though my open window and lay
across my empty bed. I lost one
and when you lose one, a little voice says, 'Hey
why not lose the other?' This is how
it becomes a streak. Did I say I lost two?
I lost three. Now I'm really boasting.
I lost one to keep the other two.
I say 'lost.' One was eaten by time.
One was lost before the curtain came up.
One I plan to find on this road.
'It took me three to know the virtue of one,'
is what I tell the barman. But I was lost
in three places. Lost once at a family Christmas,
lost twice at the dawn of my enlightenment,
lost three times by the red alarm clock
in the cupboard under the stairs of my ribs –
call it my ticker. Hang on, that makes six.
And the first loss always counts for ten.

Julia Bird

Bones

The dog done in oils to hang in the gun-room,
the one with nine shades of pink in the mouth
which never marked a shot bird's skin;

and the Scottie dog which modelled and was struck in lead
a million miniature times, each cast taken
on the same short walkies round a square of London;

and the dog wearing a bandana, framed
turning his fleas over in the long shot
concluding the coming-of-age drama,

are long gone, brought to heel by art
not knowing what it meant to be so caught.
The foxed hound sat now at my feet

is not holding out a paw for you to shake.
It barely remembers its last bone.
It barely imagines its next bone.

Rachael Boast

Coda
i.m. Manjusvara

A pen glides on its own white image
knowing nothing of it,
serving nothing but the water-music
strung from the future in the shape of a lyre.
Feathers folded, it watches the water,
that *true emblem* like a transparent sheet
spread between two realms,
respondent to everything.
Love makes us like this,
risking the second chance, defiant,
as if it were the delayed re-verb
of what we think belongs to us;
a way of being here twice,
the heart doubled in size.

Jemma Borg

A short treatise on a squid

Overhead, yes, the shark hangs
like a Renaissance saint, in whose eyes time
falls like a sediment, and no doubt
the machinations of a moray eel's jaws
are more dangerous than teeth in a glass
and it is not grief that makes the upward,
filling mass of little bells – the jellyfish –
drop again as the heart does into its sorrow,
but it's in the basement's deep and damp Atlantis,
among the transparent skins of fish,
the skeletons worn with a monstrous clarity,
that the greatest exaggeration is made
as *Vampyroteuthis infernalis* heaves into view.

That name. It reminds me of Prudentius
who said the corruption of language
is at the root of sin. Once Satan's tongue was split,
object and name slid off one another
like function and form in a tumour
or lovers making and remaking their union,
but still remaining alone. What crosses
the divide is not itself, but what has found
itself in another: an ecstasy of mind
where like is like is like. Dear metaphor
– read 'lover' – we invented heaven,
imagining sky as a fish might the land:
alien, beautiful on our tongue.

Siddhartha Bose

The Muckworm

Two warheads from Chechnya mushrooming in my hands. American
eyes bartered in gold coins. Baghdad's looted treasures in the spilt-
foam of my pocket. Chowmein cunts, hyacinth nipples, strawdog soup
from Cambodia, gashed in my neck.

My head's decked with Shanghai pearls, snakeskin jackets in
Hongkong, where ming-lords served me the keys to their kingdom
husked in the liver of a dragon.

I cruiselined my way to the Himalayas, cutting the ocean to craters.
Pashmina shawls, dogturd hash I smoked with the Taliban. They'd
green crystals dangled like demonic suns from their beards, black tar
opium, dreamsunked like stockmarket crash. I gave no one no change.

I'd caucasian bellydancers licking the welt of my heels. I vamped up
sausage palaces in Berlin, bleeding east to west. There's a checkpoint
scar on my chest with gas-chamber knives, panopticon whispers.

I waded through nuclear nights in London, where a fat man eating the
innards of a boar, drinking sewage from the city's secret rivers, taught
me the pleasures of blue rain, frog's wine. I stole his throat, his voice in
my gauche jacket, sniped the nerve-endings of his bilious ancestry.
I became the master of voices. Rats crawled in my tongue incubating
forked languages. My face morphed to a map, chock-a-blocked with
cityscape infinites. I heard dreams, my neutrons charged with new
world jazz.

I hedgefunded my path to El Dorado, whipped up desert-storm
cocktails in Manhattan, ate Rockerfeller's ghost for breakfast, puking
the yoke of his ire — I did it all, cigared like Castro, neoneyed.

O salt fuckers, shitstewed, grovelling like toads in the ooze of your
poverty, I slaved once on the intestine streets of a botched city by the
Arabian sea, carrying the weight of blackdevil cows on my back,
gunrunning for sailors, empire builders, underworld actors.

Alleyed in slumslime, edged by a skyscraper of white marble, a sheikh from the desert stuck a gun to my temple, its heat singeing my skin. He coughed, the tongue of his beard in my ear, 'recite, heathen, in the name of the prophet, and I'll give you my oil as worship.' I plunged in the holy fire, became whole. My eyes fluttered like pigeons on the skin of the graybrown sea, my body growing rich in the histories of my era.

Now, I pile up bones, govern the world, suck out the eyes of the poor. My empire is nuclear potential, my wealth a telepathic spider, webbing global dreams in proton chips. I give no one no change. I sleep the dreams of lepers, huddled alone.

Laura Bottomley

Intimate, Infinite

I, bodiced and quaffed
You, corduroyed, plaid
Showing sock.
The intimate, infinite
Trouble with the sometimes beauty
Sometimes floozy, sometimes shock of us.

You take my hand. There is biology growing
In the nail-bed. Here
Is a quick preview.
Fingers pluck at the
Laced instrument of my back
Fourteen hands tall for the highly strung.

Intimate, infinite,
You slice the whale bone with nacreous nail.
If I were a food I'd be 'what's good here?'
With dressing on the side.

Penny Boxall

What Came First

It was the first fine day.
Not even hot – just that the sky
had broken to show itself, modestly,
startlingly blue.
We watched through the high
classroom windows, the shuddering
of cloud and sky.
After break, we filed down the lane
to the burn behind the village.
It was overgrown, dank with weed,
and the trunks were mossy, moist
to the touch. Someone called us –
held a bird's nest, complete with egg,
an almost-dome inside an O.
'Look, the bird has left the edge
so neat, as if it sliced it, somehow.'
The teacher balanced it
and led us, ambassadors, back to school –
where we found the egg gone.
Emptied, the twigs and hair
were no more than a palm,

an open grasp like the one
which took mine one afternoon
and led me to the staffroom
when I cried for the end.
She handed me
a strawberry tart – said,
'He's in heaven now,' not adding,
as I thought she would,
'if there is a heaven.' I studied
the crown of berries,
their rich sauce, wondering
if I should eat it if I could not say for sure.

David Briggs

When Sam Beckett

tried travel, he went in search of
language: street-names to work into
poetry; the verb to lay as a play's
keystone. Brooding in the cheap hotels,
he'd pluck cigars from his father's
camphor box, pull on a second sweater,
crack the spines of philosophy for a fire
– sodabread crisping on a toasting fork;
his head the Tower of Babel.

And it was not unknown for Sam
Beckett to try bordellos – a different age;
a middle-class boy. What he felt as he
knocked in code on back-lane doors, or
shrugged off his jacket, hidden
somewhere in a character we're not
supposed to like, but recognise.

When Sam Beckett walked the
Händelstraße, alone in his greatcoat, to a
decadent exhibition, he noted names
and bracketed dates: so many
introductions, and disappointments:
painters whose conversations were dead
telephones; Ottoline Morrell turning up
her snub nose at a veal schnitzel.

But when Sam Beckett played piano, it
was Debussy, in the dark – hunch-
backed, planting chords in a row,
seeding the room with meaning.

And Sam Beckett knew his Bible, almost
as well as the dusty path through
Cooldrinagh that lead back to the terrain
of his fathers, where he played golf,
tocked his orb of gutta-percha about the
dips and swales of a Dublin-bay links –

his mind entering easily the requisite zone of abstraction; his wiry frame a sprung willow; the ball taking its cue, scuffling to the pre-determined point between road and yew, where it shook off its boots and waited.

Zoë Brigley

All of which are American dreams

American dreams are ill-fitting shoes that fatten
your heel to a blister. They appear as a figure
that you try to greet from a long way off; to your call,
lost in the din of the city, he never answers anything.
There are long cherished dreams that we colonize:
dreams are feathery seed pods which are borne
on the wind to catch on our sleeves, in sterile hair;
dreams are hands inked by grimy photographs
or newsprint; dreams are blazing; the land-burning
or forest fires that blacken burnished harvest plots;
dreams are flies which buzz and glint their wings gold;
they are dull vibrations entering your body through earth,
or they are a tinny song, the mumblings of a radio script
heard underwater, or from the breeze on a distant shore.

American dreams are whirring at night to shore us up
against doubt: the fears that are always fattening.
Like Fay Wray who screamed her way out of the script
of *King Kong*, dreams are shrieking: a mother bereft.
Or they silently worm their way in the tunnelled earth,
wheedling openings from the bars of every prison cell.
Their dreams infect you like the fever for gold,
though you know they'll never amount to anything.
But above all these dreams cultivate love, their plots
small among the multitude longings of the colony,
where we yearn for men or women of our dreamlands:
the passages and shafts of sleep where desire is born.
And all the lovers burning in the New World geography
dream, like you and me, of one slow, inevitable touch.

Phil Brown

Health and Safety

Do you know who I am?

Cool moody youths don't know who I am.

Pin-striped piranhas skimming through the city don't know who I am.

Cold colleagues with their coffee mugs and same spots of the staff room don't know who I am.

The worn wooden piano I press for sympathy long after it's polite to disturb one's neighbours in a sleepy suburban cul-de-sac doesn't know who I am.

Hazy homonyms designed to trick children into confusing their theres and wear on their wares through unfair fares to whole holes worn to warn that an ode is owed don't know who I am.

Gaudy logos, cheaply vectored, curned churned out to stick on a synapse cut through the crowd like cocktail party theory forcing awareness of a bland brand salting up the semantic field with crafty connotations don't know who I am.

Epic disaster movies depicting a world rubble-wrecked waterswept ice-aged concrete cracked gaping bring back the dinosaurs let them fight it out with the cockroaches for supremacy and see if the next superspecies sees it pertinent to think up names for the different types of cloud don't know who I am.

The bubbles in a poorly poured pint pinching popping tingling tongues gushing leaping lively jumping up to pop potent in the pubs eerie air open to an explosion an instant screaming at a canine frequency entering the ether awkwardly before ascending the nostrils of its next recipient running through blood at the rush of respiration finally falling out of circulation and out the ozone don't know who I am.

The paperclip-prick in Microsoft Office, bouncing around offering
unwanted help, shifting shapes and commenting on what it thinks I'm
trying to do but never really grasping my intention as I wrestle with
reluctant words and try desperately to say the things that would
express my love for Eric the paperclip gambols about the peripheries
spouting advice based on assumptions and pushes my paragraphs
around as if I asked for an indent or long for a list or begged for a
bullet-point but fuck off you don't know who I am!

Silent siblings sob and saunter at a most regrettable family reunion that
hit us all from nowhere but brought us back to a sort of solidarity in
ways that weddings or birthdays can't quite achieve and as we swap
huge and grief's platitudes and begin to divide the responsibilities
according to time location and acumen we size eachother up almost
clinically whilst huddling round a hole dug to be covered comforted
by the abundance of flowers sent from all corners of the country and I
hope I'm not crass for noticing the reserved plot to the left kept for his
other half when her time comes I know we've all noticed glancing
sympathetically to eachother consoling as best as we can without really
knowing who we are or who I am.

A box with windows that won't open fully for fear of health and safety
despite being on the ground floor full to capacity with malleable minds
of bored cranky kids clock-watching hoping for a fire drill as I drone
and drag them through a syllabus styled by those with the say so
anchoring their attention with the lights dimmed and the projector-fan
wheezing desperately for their acceptance and one wanton rebel tries
the trick of consuming a whole packet of Polos undetected while I
pontificate about the influence of other cultures on the writing of such
and such and of course I clocked him scoffing twenty minutes ago but I
relish this cat and mouse and feel that if I address it in a quiet word
after hours then perhaps he will think me more fair and pass the
sentiments onto the bigger fish and I will be heralded as the teacher
who deals justly and without prejudice with those caught eating mints
under the table and tales told of me will become legendary as all
gather round to hear of my rule-bending ways hoping to gain some
small sense of who I am.

When my elderly neighbour wants to let me know of her presence or
her discontent with the volume of my music she takes the passive
aggressive approach and spends some twenty minutes hanging a pair

of her pants on the washing line no matter the nature of the weather that day then she will slam the shed door and cough as many decibels as she can manage and I will invariably take the hint and switch to something softer and pop the sound levels down to a dull roar but then I resent her for this as her ears cannot be so sensitive if I can hear the theme from Emmerdale vibrating through my wall every evening or does she blare her soaps out of malice and is Eastenders her Elvis or is this still payback for the party I threw three Summers ago wherein a friend threw a smoked substance over her fence an offence for which I've tried in earnest to apologise buying flowers and chocolate and offering to clean away any debris through the medium of notes through the letterbox but she will never open her door no matter how many attempts made but rather peers through the mesh curtains awaiting my exit wondering who I think I am.

The burglar-sensitive security light clocks my more exaggerated movements when I theatrically flail and jump wavingly so as to have a shadow for company as I smoke and pace the patio replaying the day's mistakes and triumphs making a tally of my standing reflecting on how to turn next week into a victory with the careful application of an ethos adopting the motto that there are lessons in defeat but I still succumb to the temptation to send petty text-messages on occasion or lash out at lost loves but then isn't that something we all do and are these flawed moments not what make us beautiful or is that the self-comforting of a hopeless man who hasn't read half the books he owns or understood half the books he's read or admitted to half the oversights he oversaw should he boil these ideas into a punchy blog post or a cool comment on somebody else's or is this feeling best saved for a status update to be read and interpreted by close friends estranged acquaintances colleagues old teachers school-friends or increasingly commonly friends of friends who may have met you or have a feeling they may like to or briefly admired the wit of a wall post left on a mutual friend before adding you to find you an overwhelming let-down but the act of removing an e-friend is a deeply political manoeuvre and leaves one open to more attack and demand of justification than it is often worth and so we linger on eachother's social spheres clogging up news-feeds and inviting eachother to all manner of allegiances and gatherings despite the fact that we've never met and you've no idea who I am.

Mark Burnhope

The Centre
for Graham

Christ is not your friend our lecturer said.
His evidence: ring-binder thin, but Lord,

we believed him. *I came not to bring peace,*
but the sword. Not to unite, but to divide.

*

Boscombe Pier pierces

the sea. On either side of me
the promenade extends

arms that end
in bending wrists of cliff-side.

The land is dark, but look, his fists
pin-lit,

loosing breakers overnight.

Jenna Butler

Telling It Slant

In memory, Robert Kroetsch and Muriel Butler
For Jim

'It is not the dead that dying hurts most.'
'I love words and therefore I am a liar.' – John Newlove

It's too easy to blame these halfwit words,
their gorgeousness and rumpled ease
unfolding like birds, like long-limbed sylphs.
Their hunger to ensure the proper tale,
their open-armed desire to please.

The trick's in how you wear them; if
you let each poem turn to lie –
a riff on the same old heartbreak tune –
or bleed out all that crippled dark
and splay them open to rain and sky.

And what I'm trying to say is this:
love comes and leaves in equal measure;
what's ever missed, what's newly found;
the heart finds balance in constant shift,
finds refuge in the thought of weather.

James Byrne

No Smoking

Pulling away residually from old devotions,
I keep my brow low and watch the domino
bones capsize: encoded snow on black slate.
Falling, the equation misses my forebrain—
its inventorying of the foamy bar menu,
divided / sub-divided by the burly ruckus
where a man smokes from his supernatural
mouth and another coupons the jukebox
with charred screams. The falcon landlord
flashes at my hard-bitten nails, a combustible
look. He's a gimcrack, menacing the anecdotes,
sure that mine will brink me out and over—
outsider to the unspillable smile of the maitre d'
who asks 'what will it be?' and cannot tell me.

Christian Campbell

At Buckingham Palace

I

I am the first of my family
to go to Buckingham Palace.
I had the flu, I nearly stayed home;
left my hair in all its might,
wore a beige linen suit.

Her Majesty was in a red dress
with horrid black gloves,
her hair like rigor mortis.
This was not the White House.
She was very, very calm.

Van Dyck, Rubens,
Rembrandt, Canaletto
from all angles, oil paintings
on the ceilings and walls. The eyes
of Anglo nobles glaring down,
draperies, mirrors and all.
Sèvres porcelain, Canova
and Chantrey sculpture,
servants, secret rooms,
French furniture.
But no crown jewels
from India in sight,
none from Benin.

Mister, Mister,
where have you been?
I been to London
to see the Queen.

Some of the ladies curtsied,
some of the men bowed.
The Queen raised her black glove
high (as with rings and bent wrists)
and I received the Royal Chalice:

Light up your spliff,
Light up your chalice,
Make we smoke it inna
Buk In Hamm Palace.

II
The Queen came to Nassau
when I was eight.
The whole family walked
to streets lined like Boxing Day,
to see her pass in a green Jaguar,
to see that white-gloved wave
borrowed in pageants, float parades.

Benjamin Zephaniah, Rasta poet,
turned down the OBE. *Up yours,*
he said, *No way Mr. Blair, no way Mrs. Queen.*
When my grandfather got that MBE,
name blazing on the Queen's
New Year's Honors List,
Her Majesty told him something
that he would stage for guests
for years, displaying his medal
as a child shows a good wound.
Wear your best suit, he would have said,
Make sure cut your hair, shine up
your shoes.

Niall Campbell

July, Snow Clouds

Back then, the thinnest boy in school
had disclosed how he'd lost a summer
spraying WD-40 on stale bread,

scattering this for the porch birds.
How he'd watch as mid-flight, or dive,
or song, they suddenly would open

from themselves like a solved knot.
My childhood earned disbelieving him.
This sky cold, quiet, he's recalled,

his pale hands, long as a night awake,
and realised in his father's shed;
white under-feathers in the air.
A snow-fall in the height of summer.

Vahni Capildeo

& The Frame Said

Now and then, on the telephone,
you carry news to me of me;
glad-voiced, having kept the bread,
handing over daffodils,
rushing like love told by armfuls,
say you've been where they asked for me.
But I had not asked, I had not
been asked: your rich, fractional life
cooled into halves and other halves…
Sleep has run into my ankles.
Water rising lilac-eyed,
my tongue raises a cairn of pebbles.
I care not whence you spring your smiles,
or to place tall vases on tables.

Melanie Challenger

Gott Bay, or Salvation

'Θυμήσου, σώμα...

Σώμα, θυμήσου όχι μόνο το πόσο αγαπήθηκες...
αλλά κ' εκείνες τες επιθυμίες που για σένα
γυάλιζαν μες στα μάτια φανερά.'

Body, remember not only how much you were loved...
But also those desires that glowed openly
In eyes that looked at you.

— Constantine Cavafy, 'Body, Remember'

Body, remember against this priggish darkness.
Only remember the unsubstantiated
Of our primitive clutch, the prey of old desire
Deadlocked at our feet. The skelves of lapwings mourn us,
Their crested forgotten fingers wag in the night.
As Christly images, let our relic organs piece
Together the landscape. Let our entrails bleat
The wild and our gullets preach the oceanbed. *Wight,*
Remember the suns whose singular glance
Ripened and sprung us. Your eyes as my suns,
And my spring chorus as the night cannibalises
The sly, raptorial light debauching the air between us.
Open your eyes now to this darkness.
Here are the soft levels; the sea; the shale:
Breast the current: your body shall renew as the eagle.

John Challis

Jazz Maggot

I

The lure, in that writhing red dress flicks back
and forth provocatively before the sleek
silvery breams, caught between sun flutter
and disco flicker, on the scales of their fresh
pressed tonic suits and combed fin.
They will grope at you maggot, leer
with an amber eye and bend slug coloured water
around you maggot. They come flee circle,
nuzzle you with thin brim of nose maggot,
tease and tow you in waltz, thin blue lips close
to your small face maggot. They are wanton
pushing each other aside, knocking you
in red heels to a stumble. You are ripe,
gaping, like a pomegranate, maggot.

II

But they don't know you wear a wire maggot?
Recording each offence with subtle
tugs of distress, an alarm calling to father,
as they rub the red garment from you,
sifting the dye from your skin with their scales,
nibbling behind your ears (if you had them)
silently tonguing the slug of water
that surrounds you maggot. It is too late,
the sharp restraint pulled as he takes you
into his arm jaw. You burst for him,
underneath that writhing red dress
he is crack-jawed in admiration,
he savours your final dance steps along
his thorny throat. He will die for you maggot.

John Clegg

Seasons in the Frame Shop

I work in the frame shop that uses willow.
Different frame shops use different woods
which each have their strengths and weaknesses:
pine is especially cheap, balsa is pliant,
cedar- and sandal-wood frames can differentiate
photos of wives from photos of mistresses.
Willow is used for abstract art and found objects.
I suffered as a child from epileptic seizures
which left me with an aversion to abstract art,
nonetheless I do as good a job on the frames
as I can. I love willow. I wouldn't frame
with anything else if I was given the choice.
I tune my hand in calibration with the grain,
if I touch an inch of willow-branch I could tell you
the shape of the tree and all its faultlines
which serve to make the individual frame unique.
My shop's on a quiet sub-alley; days or more
pass without custom, my grin in all the mirrors.
When I carve willow, I'm the end of the world.

Ross Cogan

Zelda in the Asylum

I am in the world to do something unusual, extraordinary.
– Zelda Fitzgerald

Believe it beloved. Eighteen, trembling
at the high board; below, the cool blue pool
settles like a picnic spread. *I've got
my fingers crossed.* I walk brightly along
in high places. The smell of motor oil
and jazz mingles slickly in the night streets,
gets in my hair, my clothes; my hips are wild
tonight – you don't mind do you? *Sweetie pie.*
I was the girl with orange blossoms, dancing
in the fountains, the streets: The Monkey Glide,
Cakewalk, The Black Bottom – Armstrong's Hot Five
crackling on a wind-up gramophone. *Let's sing
again.* It's hot tonight. The world's so full
the colour's slipped its moorings, joined the air
like a tune refusing to be locked up
in bars. I chase it with my paints. *What will
I do in the morning?* A salamander
that's what I longed to be. Coolly to step
slick from the fire that chased us round the Dome,
to the Select, the Dingo, the Rotônde,
the Viking, sure as the diver poised above
the long fall. Even Paris palls in time.
All my life. Good for nothing but love.

Jane Commane

Coventry is

You know, Wordsworth said of Coventry that it was one of the most beautiful cities in all of England. It is a pity… a great pity.

from *One Night in November*

always the bridesmaid and never the bride,
     somewhere to be sent,

where you come to find your train of thoughts
     and miss the last train home,

where things come to end and the opening paragraph
     is rewritten, then lost, then bodged,

where hope is exchanged for something a little less brash,
     like *maybe, perhaps,*

an ugly/beautiful place that seeks someone
     to love it back,

missing the letters you used to write home
     and wishes you would call,

preferring not to talk, tonight, of the masses buried
     at London Road, the dead car plants,

much maligned, rarely loved, occasionally
     extra-marital, a clandestine affair,

too old and worn out for *that* kind of
     funny business,

disgusted, outraged at the suggestion and only needs
     a good architect to get rid of the dark roots,

wants you to know that she didn't always
     look this way,

going to raise a little soul and get herself
     back on that bloody horse.

Swithun Cooper

The Electric City

The blinking high-rise opposite our room
        illuminates a heated nylon couch,
a sheetless mattress, ventilators, chrome.

        A woman yawns; a man figures a switch.
We watch the dimming contours of their forms
        until we cannot tell which one is which.

Sarah Corbett

Breaking Horses

1
My love of horses comes down
on my father's side, through his father's father.
There's a photograph, lost now too,
of the cabbie in his coat and whiskers

holding the head of a tall gelding
in its upright shoes, the tied-in fetlocks
and roughed up cannon bones
those old cab horses always seem to show.

The story goes how the old man
whipped a driver known for his cruelty,
brought him to his knees in the street,
a long flick and smack about the neck

as their cabs passed. With this for pride
I was both tethered to the post
of my ancestor and sent skittering on
like a yearling with its rump slapped.

2

My last summer at home thirteen mountain ponies were found, ruined,
but still alive, in a quarry above Caerwys, their lips cut off at the teeth,
their ears close to their heads, their eyelids cut to the bone, as
Evnissyen did to the horses of the King of Ireland. What had they been
brought to witness, these thirteen? Their fetlocks had been tied, and
they lay tethered on their sides, eyes back to the white, a row of
grimaces. The local news was full of it, and there was a general outcry,
talk of ritual and spell, of something risen that had long lay buried.

3

Dostoevsky knew. It took three pages
to mark the death of that horse
whipped to its knees in the dream,
the small boy Raskolnikov holding
all that time his mother's hand,
this one anchor tying him to the horror,
pushing it back somewhere – into his mouth,
behind his teeth and tongue – the hungry
cells of his brain opening a snap
then shuttering on the tiny upturned picture.

I lay on my bed in the early evening
unaware of the darkening tablet of window,
the lights flicking on a mile across the estuary
and the night birds setting out.
I read like this for weeks all summer
and the walls held in that small room
like a drawing of a girl reading,
her mind an open mouth, an unfed hunger,
the broken horse and the inaudible snap
of the rope inside her.

Emily Critchley

To his Uncool Mistress [after Marvell]

Had I but half a wit & space in which
Personal ambition didn't saturate everything
I did or sought to do; were I a man,
For whom love studied & love unattained
Was less vivid, resounded less than the *real thing*;
I'd sit & think & walk & pass my days
With you in true mutual bliss. We'd be
To each other the pearls & rubies I hunt out
In books & hoard for my own mind's sake. I'd fancy
Myself less a complainer, a hungerer after
Renaissance fashion, that needs no real finishing
From you ~ except as a prize worthily won;
A jewel, the chasing after which, once gained,
Gratified my seedier parts in self-intoxicating
Lustre ~ my heart might really grow.
        And never mind the Flood, we've save *each other*
        From this world's weary transience.

I'd care less for your eyes, your face, your figure,
& the parts all vegetable loves sustain,
& try to offer you instead the rate
        At which you should really be valued. For lady,
        Love should be exchanged only for love.

Alas, when I had all eternity
To chase, to muse, & wonder at my own
Self-worth; to seek for higher things whose sheen
Might give me that vicarious glow I crave ~
That which might make me look *really good* ~
You gave it up. And in so doing spoilt
The game in which you *were* the game, & I ~
The hunter, fainting after you, foot-sore
& heart-depressed with weary hunger. I

Would have been the only worm to try yr long-
Preserved virginity. Imagine my
Surprise when, with a light yielding, you,
An amorous bird of prey, turned to me
With equal hunger & a need to share
Such love-pleasure on a level footing.
The tamed grown tamer! No, it couldn't be.
     Your little ball once rolled & offered isn't
     Quite the same at all.

Thus I alone now face those gates of life,
Content myself with their impressive height,
Desire to be the one brave lover-of-himself
To try to penetrate their mystery; conquer,
     Or to still die trying.

Abi Curtis

Thought Bubble

I look above and see it resting on the ceiling:
glassy, tissue-thin and supple, issuing

from three full-stops dreamt up in foam,
like the stuff we used to lag the loft.

A bulbous, old-style telly, diver's helmet, that fishbowl
we've had no use for, since Jaffa passed away.

It takes some time to realise that it's mine.
I know because it follows the movement of my head

as I wander 'round the flat, connected
by the kind of loops we finger on the telephone.

I feel beside myself, beneath the shadow
of a milky cave, a chamber of echoes.

I've batted it softly with my fingertips,
wrapped a scarf to blot its straining eye,

touched its slick surface to my lips.
It quietly squeaked, but all its sudsy links

still grip me like a weightless chain.
How do I explain this gently bobbing drop?

You're far too bright for lies about experiments
with paper shades and helium.

When you return I'll have to hide it in the curtains,
standing nonchalant, or hold it squirming in my lap.

Scenes reel across its haunted skin.
Should you discover it, I fear

you'll make it burst
in tiny tributaries whose passing

sounds like laughter,
or weeping.

Rishi Dastidar

22 March, Working in an Office on Berners Street

It is four days and half an average lifetime
after a simile happened to Richard Brautigan

elsewhere, half an ocean away.
Nothing has happened to me

except that the sun has come out
for the first time in my life,

the way the light comes on when you open
a fridge, and two slices of last night's pizza

are waiting to be breakfasted upon.
In 38 years time, the Met Office and the news app

won't be able to tell you what happened but trust me,
it's as true as the expression on your face right now.

Amy De'Ath

Tall Glass

So you are
the clearest, loneliest
tall glass, and you
are free, and you
are paler to me than
a milieu of pale
teenage girls scrubbing,
condensing massively
into a huge
tear, you are
the advert for
the glass you
are drinking
from, is this
the glass you are
drinking from, is
this that glass,
does it trouble you
the ages
the day you were
eaten in
French, the myth
of the social volcano
being a girl
do you think happiness
like a small
bird or balloon
is available only to us –
some birds will
be here long
after I'm dead.
I'd like to
unbind a couple
of climates
and I do,
rolling around
in the sweatpools

from your
forehead. There is
a difference between
me and you
a good reason to
swap saliva, or for
you to describe
yourself from
over there, then
move
quickly away
Yes but you
do not have to
the huge baby
of spring is
bouncing towards us
about to cast
his reckoning on
our heads and
decide we are all right
to go on
living if we
like, hope leaning
on the air between
tenements, holy
mother of snow
I miss you –
altitude of bees, tall
scarf a richness I know,
I will be
there too
in the glass
there is such
a richness.

Antony Dunn

Self-Portrait in Betty's Café Tea Room, Ilkley

He should know better than to face himself
into a mirrored corner, in his state.

He has a poet's eye and by the time
the tea-things are arrived and set out straight

he's gone and memorised the whole damn room –
found himself, no less, at the cooling end

of a minuscule affair of glances
with a harassed mother several tables off.

I know. I've been studying in the glass
how he's so intimately learned his place

that when he stands, turns out to face the world
he'll find it, staggered, all the wrong way round,

upset some tables, spill apologies
to folk he does and doesn't recognise.

Joe Dunthorne

All my friends regardless

All my friends regardless,
come to my garden and pretend to get along.
Please let me introduce the scientists. Yes,
he studies the behaviour of bees.
Friends from my childhood,
I do not think you stupid and boring.
Assistant editors, step away from the pond.
This man has written a dystopian
sci-fi novel; this man is an eco-carpenter.

I am on the roof, feeling so various,
astonished by my own width,
with water bombs in each hand.

Rhian Edwards

Hunch

My mouth has been falling to pieces again.
I've been Sellotaping the faults,
making a blur of my conversations,
drawing lines where they ought to be.

I'm procrastinating in the bathroom again,
shirking the relentless constant of bedtime
where you will be patient or cruel. Can I
get up now, even though it's still dark?

The hunch has come crawling back.
Is it because I've been living in my throat
and trembling at every kindness?
One day I'll cry and make a sound.

Michael Egan

john dolphin

I can't tell you much about john dolphin
other than how I'd been told that he was born not long before me
with a porpoise's head   how apart from that he was a normal child
but his mother could never hold him and no home would ever take
     him

how he lived on that peninsula of land beyond the river
where norse-blooded bandits once shut off that border bulwark
spike of bee-stung finger stiffly aware of the touch of too near digits
caught there   jutting in wait of the throb's subsidence

how john dolphin made a home on a pebbled beach
where seaweed snaked between smoothed gaps
and hermit crabs drifted in scraped out rock pools
how he jealously watched those easy to home wanderers

how he'd sit on the dunes at sun's rising and setting as shelducks flew
     to hoylake
and he'd feel the wind shift the sand and watch how the year's ebbing
froze the marram and lyme grass to brittle blades as deep-water
     drowning natterjacks
in cacophonous harmony trilled a chorus that carried his forgotten
     mother's cooing

how one day I saw him standing over a dead portuguese man o'war
as I reached a cove of cliff-touching sand and pebble from where I
     couldn't go on
so turning I saw his ever-wet and silver-grey head held low and empty
     eyed
taking in the slab of broken pier wall that had caved in that jelly fish

how he was wearing outgrown and tattered jeans marred with sea-
    grime
and decorated with sewn on cockle and hydrobia shells hanging by
    hornwrack threads
how he knelt then and that his chest was bare and with his porpoise
    jaw opening
he lifted the stone and tossed it aside back to the incoming tide as a
    godwit cried

how he carefully began to peel away the seaweed that had embedded
    in the lump
then closing his comb toothed mouth he laid his hand on the wrecked
    caravel
and as he knelt in his reverence I climbed the dunes away from the fast
    returning water
that lapped around him like he was a rock a shell a part of the shore
    caught detritus

how he didn't move as the sea swallowed the day beneath a tyrian
    darkened horizon
and let the water lap at his shell covered jeans   rise to his sand
    yellowed chest
how I turned away and didn't watch as he was cradled by his salt-wet
    mother's embrace
as his tide returned for him and his murmurs echoed out into the sea.

Inua Ellams

Snipers and Porcupine Quills

One
A folk story goes that two porcupines, Goliaths
of their tribes, clashed at dawn. Fairly matched
neither waned till the truce at dusk, shrugged
off their coat of thorns and from opposite sides
paddled a soothing pool, colliding in the middle.
Naked, vulnerable, both reached for razor reeds
until the half-moon lit their tired limbs, showed
each other's chests: a nest of scar tissue. It's said
this cleared their heads of war and together, left
the battle, not a ripple, not a word.

Two
Sierra Leone's civil war reeks of rape and rebels,
fields of widowed women, scorched flesh, torn
necks and entire villages hacked off like limbs.
Unlikely it seems that anything paused the gun-
toting cut throats and mercenaries. But a bar
named Paddy's, its arms-free zone, its dance
floor thick with cheap quick liquor for raiders,
traitors, loyalists and mavericks; the conflict
left with weapons outside, piled for the rustle
and ripple of leaves.

Three
I could quote any: Iraq, Afghanistan, Rwanda,
Northern Ireland, Brixton's riots, street wars,
all the moulds of soldier taught the bay of blood.
I could conjure you a sniper perched stonestill,
mouth a pool of prayers, finger flicking trigger,
could paint a splattered skull but for my dream
of time, of silence, thought, clear talk and
gun muzzles cooling like porcupine quills.

Lamorna Elmer

Strange Fidelities

This morning you caught me off centre:
holding a fan to my face and saying,
This is the colour of your lips – must you bite them?
I stuttered, looking down at the garden's bright grass,
wanting you to draw the fan's edge
against my cheek, leave an imprint on my skin,
exposing my ECG terrain.
Years previously, when I was new to Osaka
and around by authority I'll sprinkled bathwater over your hair
in the lukewarm light of a hotel bathroom.
You were sharpening knives, telling me
The Japanese are the best at torture.
Back then I was sharper to your needs.
I thought of others, iodine-skinned women
lithe as pins, legs filmed by mink stockings.
One came to the house on Saturday. I'd cooked – you
were sampling English cuisine, dipping roast potatoes
in gravy and feeding me chunks before tasting them
yourself. You got off on suspicion.
We sat for three hours in front of the television
as you told her of my talents, simmering
with laughter. I went out to sit on the porch and smoke.
The woman's name was Hashizume, she told me
as she left. I become obsessed with her feet,
following her veins up to her ankles. She waved
a banknote by way of explanation.
The stake that sticks out gets hammered down,
she said, which surprised me, and then didn't.
The women I met in the months that followed
mainly wanted to discuss cookery, ways to cure fish.
Had I a snakeskin nailed to a doorframe? one asked.
And yet, this morning in the garden
you tell me you have heard of wives like me.
Wives that stand and act like shadows, marking calendars
with crosses, beginning the thirty year countdown
until we ourselves are bathed in silver.

Andrew Fentham

XL

The year Caligula appointed his horse
to the senate began on a Friday,
was a leap year known by a different name.
In Alexandria Mark was in discourse
on a new see, ushering Coptics the way
to a God and calendar that were the same.
Later when drawing up his Easter table
the small monk Dionysius in his cell
would use the Roman system of numerals
to rename that year Anno Domini XL.

At the fourth iteration we begin
to subtract and meet L at two score,
the number of many, a generation
or estimate. Soldiers of the Sanhedrin
would spare a sinner the fortieth scourge;
forty years the rule of Kings Saul, Solomon,
Eli and David; for forty days and nights
Christ roamed the limestone Quarantal lands,
or later as holy zombie before alight
at, restoration to, the Right Hand.

Forty is discrete, a natural reckon
alphabetised by a faint contraction
before the historic r, pseudoperfect;
two and a half ordinations of chessmen:
seven queens have forty solutions.
The marriage of Celsius and Fahrenheit
at forty below is a cold mirror
to the patterning of the double digit,
octagonal cardinal integer
with the mathematics of God in it.

And yet forty is domestic, life's deuce –
at best a ruby wedding in faithful clutch,
more usually an approaching hill,
a speed limit or reappraisal of use,
a few winks or a working week as much
as a new waist size, the flabby middle
of the song, the moving hammy chorus
offering a new look at a life riven
by our own choices, or those made for us,
the forty acres and a mule never given.

S.J. Fowler

(Steggr)

a rattle whittled from an antler
the animal had fallen by the road
dead of starvation
the brown needle nittle
could be hewn or settled
with string or gut from the same carcass
instead it was placed point-first
beneath the fingernail of Ivan
and edged beneath
tick by tick
until he shared his secret
or fainted from the pain
we learned which herbs were poison
which rivers ran north
we learned the lathe of magnetism
and salves
made of mud and roots rotting
put to use as glue
to replace a fingernail, severed
now black in water's blue

{this is the Stag}

Alexander Freer

An Affair in Four Parts

1

The dry days come. An unexpected frost,
a slew of dead leaves. Winter's early nights set
bodies in darkness, vicious and suggestible.
We are at those dangerous margins
of sleep where anything can be true.

2

Sure as morning the feeling climbs.
Stiff routine, the long *erfahrung*
is not enough. There is a gap
in the day which remains
unanswerable and it is shaped
like you. Bodies tend to resist
only so long. Either you will snare me
or I will snare you, my dear one.

3

Passion summons action, as angels
appear to those who fiercely desire.
Stripping away context, residues
and clothes we become ourselves,
here in the negative we sculpt this love.
I grapple for a backwards Christ
renouncing the world for your flesh.

4

The way our limbs function
to speak our desires, or lie
like a web of empty signifiers,
anonymous and lovely,
as we sleep so close,
labouring for the delicate
ignorance of strangers.

Isabel Galleymore

Fishing

When she puts the lid on the ice-cream box
half-full with the pink and writhe of worms
she presses each corner until plastic meets
plastic with a satisfying click. She asks herself
have I been dreaming?
All day she's repeated the same question so
when sleeping tonight she'll be in the rhythm
of asking again – have I been dreaming?
and she can say yes. This, she's been told,
will let her harness the dream's direction
but she's not experienced much success yet.
She sees the line tug so directs her focus
to draw up the weight the hook holds in the water
to find she's caught Elvis holding a bright, beautiful lettuce.

Alan Gillis

The Debt Collector

Between the anticipation and aftermath,
the trickle of water and quenching of thirst;
between the wish and what comes out in the wash,
the seed packet and gladioli bloom;
between now, then and when,
all that you know will vanish down the plug hole.

No matter how ripe the fruit in the bowl,
erotic the violets, erratic the stars,
at night empty rooms gather you in their claws.
Their silence licks you. All that is lost,
all that is botched streams into one strange image
in the mirror and speaks with your voice.

Darker by the day, you feel a stranger
hover at the window, eavesdrop on your calls,
at your shoulder in darkened corridors,
head-bowed two seats ahead of you on the bus,
in the shade of the lindens and silver limes,
adept and ready, wearing white gloves.

On a bare wall the clock-face ticks.
That you were never liable is a myth
like easy money. So live accordingly.
The hours are long, the months disappear,
and the moment nears when he will come.
He will have your eyes.

Only if you're lucky will he come quietly,
steal into your borrowed home and lead you
from dreaming loves, through this town's coil
of limbs and longing, bear you through the rain,
along nameless roads to a green wood
whose river weaves its murmur with conifer song.

There he will lay you down in the riverweed,
clubmoss, hazel scrub, milkweed, witch butter,
covered in a shallow night of crawling soil.
So make the most of your loan, though all that
is gone, or is going, will never let you go.
In our deaths our debt will grow.

James Goodman

Hensbarrow

buzzard in the sky—driftwood—feathers salt-worn—trailing in the
airstream—its body pebbled by the flow—

ocean fragments both sides of the moor—sea bluer than before,
solid blue—keeping watch, waiting—

moorland in-between—sweep of heather and gorse—wide white
tracks—squabbling clutch of cottages—white crossroads—high,
dark thirsty lines of hedges—

scribbling motor noise in the pitworks below—lunar effacement—
the invisible gape of Littlejohns, Gunheath—

Carrancarrow's mountain of dirty salt—the tideline of black gorse
and clitter—the grim reflection of sky—

the buzzard taloned—showing its scarlet mew—distant *killas* gaudy
in the sun—tiny bright hedges and farms

Kélina Gotman

Jeff Bridges

Scruffily strutting
up from the Cave Man's
Lair

Gleaming eye
flash of a Tooth

Certain

of his certainty

in War, and Gymnastics

in the pentatonic flute

in the reconstructed pelt.

Kathryn Gray

Testament

O Brandon, my brown-eyed boy, I will not answer
critics who say you're a triumph of style over substance
and that your lyrics do not make grammatical sense.
I tell you now: I have known, myself, such an audience.
And when I listened to your solo effort, *Flamingo*,
I wept for that part of their heart that would not hear,
wept for that part of your heart that wept for them.
I was glad you maintained the talents of Stuart Price.

Brandon, in our early days, when first I googled you
hourly, I will confess I feared you'd disappoint me
because you were too pretty. But then I read you were
a Mormon and, though you found it difficult, you rarely
took a drink or smoked a cigarette. There again,
I must admit the fact you had a wife to whom you are,
at present, faithful, and who is the mother of your three
children, dealt a blow of not inconsiderable proportion.

I cannot decide, Brandon, how I like you best, just as
you cannot decide how best you like yourself. There is,
for example, that latter Americana shot through
with a dash of Bryan Ferry. Or your neophyte's tribute
to Robert Smith of The Cure, which made me rethink
men wearing eyeliner. And let us not forget your complex
relationship with facial hair, as mocked by Neil Tennant:
the baby-smooth, the bearded or my sweet bandito.

When I read how you grew in the dust bowl of sin.
When I read how, by some coincidence the stars really
fixed for us, you listened in your room to The Cars
through the hell of your teenage years, you opened, softly,
the girl in me. Brandon, it is only by a twist of Bowie
on a stereo that you did not turn golf pro, these words are
written, and the film will not carry Charlize Theron
with her katana back into the white dot of oblivion.

And when I consider such things, such things.
Brandon, Brandon, even there, in your name, flowers.

Matthew Gregory
from *Hermione and Frog*

Snails

The bedclothes were turned inside out
and the room began to flutter.

Bewilderment was a big-footed bird
whose feathers floated onto their pillow.

Hermione was quietly sobbing
into one hand inked by her eyelids,

frog was unspeaking. His tongue
had curled round such odd shapes,

sherbets of language that thrilled at first
then thickened, turned in the throat.

But Hermione had only cried softly
then took his spite respectfully,

the strings of his gibes somehow
joined to her silence across the room.

He thought of the snails he used to eat,
their eye-sprouts unfolding and recoiling

on his tongue as if they burnt.

Neil Gregory

Cortège

Two black horses
feathered like cabaret girls
high-kneeing into the road
followed by a bloom wrapped
casket of mirrored wood
and a seeming endless
string of gleaming
chassis, keening
ιιl ιlιι lιιιριιιf ιlιρlι
first gears
holding the road
and me for a brief lifetime

When they pass
I wish I'd counted
the cars

Jen Hadfield

Prenatal Polar Bear

He hangs in formaldehyde
like a softmint or astronaut
dreaming in his moonsuit –
a creased, white world.

His paws are opalescent
and dinted with seedclaws –
the flattened, unripe,
strawberries-of-the-snows.

Nathan Hamilton

Malcolm Administered

difficult   as in a black box in a dark bar   Malcolm
battles admin in the morning   unhappy rain sent
by data gods growing up bad business   their sick words

smudge Malcolm's forearm misty in a solo   stagger him
till he fluffs his notes and stumbles in his lines
all he wishes   a sturdy bench at night in gardens

to sit and be like other people   lively and with ending
but something has happened somewhere   a hardy friend
may have swung a punch

Malcolm springs back   it must be stopped
made error   questing now   dark eyes
well darker in a violent light of thinking

Sophie Hannah

The Dalai Lama on Twitter

We do as much harm to ourselves and to others when we take offence
as when we give offence.

I am following the Dalai Lama on Twitter
But the Dalai Lama is not yet following me.
That's fine. Things are as they are. I do not feel bitter.
Enlightenment is his thing. Reciprocity?
Not so much. He is a spiritual big-hitter
And I write detective novels. It's easy to see
Why I'm following the Dalai Lama on Twitter
And the Dalai Lama is not yet following me.

He doesn't know how often I pick up litter,
How many signed books I have given away for free,
Not to Russell Brand, Wayne Rooney or Gary Glitter
But as raffle prizes for this or that charity,
And since I would hate to think of myself as a quitter –
Because I, at least, know it isn't all about me –
I am following the Dalai Lama on Twitter
Even though he is self-absorbed to the Nth degree.

You'd think a sage of his rank would know about karma,
About courtesy, and the decent thing to do.
Oh, follow me, follow me, follow me, Dalai Lama!
I'm an expert on *House MD* and crime fiction too.
I wouldn't DM you outlandish theories of Dharma
Or make you retweet my latest good review.
I am following, on Twitter, the Dalai Lama
But the Dalai Lama has not thought to follow me too.

(PS – Eckhart Tolle, this also applies to you.)

A. F. Harrold

Takeaway

Waiting for my order in the takeaway
I can't help but overhear the little West Indian guy
(flat cap, squashed face, big tight voice)
bitching to the old white guy who said,
'I lost *my* wife to cancer a year ago...'
at the start of the conversation and nothing more.

It's a catalogue of misdiagnoses and misdirection,
of a lack of shared information,
of radio- and chemo- and bad results.
('She...' this, and 'She...' that. *His* wife I guess.)
The nerves get burnt out, but no one had said.
He's close to breaking up.
I hear the wobble through the rich patois roll.

I huddle behind the *TLS*,
pretend to read a poem I can't keep a grip on.
He's got me almost in tears myself,
and I want to kneel down with him and say, 'I know'.
But I don't know.
An orphan's different to a husband on the precipice.

'She wanted to have her feet washed,'
he went on, letting the darkness out through cracks,
'but there was no one...'

Oli Hazzard

Apologia

His stillness knows exactly what it wants. Flemish, it climbs
down the rungs of its laughter, til strasse-light chokes
in the key of its throat, or a reticulated fog catches
in the youngish trees; or, through the milk-bottle glaucoma
of a villainous monocle, it scouts out the gallery of a plot-hatchery
with a test-tube full of bewitching molecules. Thwarted! In the long
      hiss of its head,
thawing silence slakes the fossilising song *Their Life is Hidden with God.*

Some song! Like a soft cymbal it shirrs in the recollection.
The city's plushness crab-hands along the neck
of its buildings. Who trusts such plushness, huh? (Does *who* fuck?)
It neither declares intentions nor inters declensions.
Playing it backwards reveals a song being force-fed itself (the *tack-tock-*
      tuck-tick
of drool from its mouth). Scuppered, he lounges against the scene-
      stripping
window: tries to name, then count, then watch, the flux of birds
      palpitating

in the sprained lens of a lake, a jigsaw shaken out of its box,
indicating, in a shaky hand, that the shape's clear, the picture less so.
Cheap tricks earn cheap treats, *brother,* he mutters, before, like the
      sudden urge to
feign sleep, an obscure and untrustworthy impulse selects
the sensation, then turns it over to itself: do what you have to,
      (Baltimore, *simpatico*)
but make it quick. But his stillness could outrun itself. Decades without
      water!
Then: We don't seem to have moved. *Then*: Every move an altar.

Lindsey Holland

Spiked

And then there's the day when a fast squirrel drops
strange nuts into the birdbath. They dissolve

so by the time the mist has milked itself clear
nothing seems unusual. The sundial still

predicts a western morning and pink feet ignore
the numb stone, beaks split the surface

tension, no greater or lesser than yesterday, and tongues
like computer-weary fingers feel their way

to nourishment. From a summer thick
branch in the alder tree, dark worlds watch

each plump body topple and smack the paving slabs.
There is no point in this. But if you listen

you'll hear the rustling, rodent mouths chattering
like men in a bar as another girl loses herself.

Matthew Hollis

The Diomedes

Summers he would leave for Alaska,
working the crabbers as deckhand or galley;
autumns returning with cold-weather stories of
clam catchers, fur trappers, and the twin isles
of Diomede: two miles and a continent between them;
and how, in winter, when the straits froze over,
the islanders could walk from one to the other,
crossing the ice-sheet to see family, swap
scrimshaw, the season's stories, or marry,
passing the Date Line that ran through the channel,
and so stepping between days as they went.

As far as I know he never went back;
if he had he'd have learned that
only the bravest now track on foot,
the winter ice no longer reliable,
for walrus, ski-plane or the human step,
leaving the skin boats alone to wait for the summer,
to edge themselves into the melt-water.

Even now, there's something to his story
I find difficult to fathom. At home, in London,
listening to my neighbours' raised voices,
or catching the girl opposite dressing,
I wonder, what it is we will do to be neighbourly,
how part of us longs for it to matter that much,
to be willing to nudge our small boat into the waves,
or set foot on the winter ice,
to be half-way from home, in no safety,
unsure if we're headed for tomorrow or yesterday.

Wayne Holloway-Smith

Cutting a Figure

Begin by losing yourself.
Burn your old clothes, your love notes.
Sit naked at your midnight window,
weighing the cadence of the age.

Become a flicker behind the blue smoke
of dive bars. Decipher conversations,
eavesdrop on topics that hold attention:
plot the growth of future trends.

Memorise turns of phrase
and adapt their use for other circles.
Survey the movement of masters;
scrutinize your artful ancestors –

Brummel, Langtry – trace and retrace
their images. Mimic the mannerisms
of success, as the apprentice does
before he attempts the autonomous stroke.

Etch an outline of your ideal.
Let it hold you accountable.
Feign authenticity, be well versed
in the art of telling a lie. Examine

the parameters of social acceptance;
be scandalous within. Allow yourself
to be held but not bridled.
Perhaps then you will be ready to emerge

in society, to court the light, to have
your features captured in photographs,
your exploits noted in memoirs
you'll one day strike a match to.

Holly Hopkins

Margaret and her Cottage, Ontario

You're swimming across the lake on steel hips,
your basalt bones had quite worn down
and with your new motor you're kicking to the island,
keeping your head up and dry, facing down the floating birds.

Behind you the boathouse is stark,
its bright pine has not yet settled into the landscape.
Last year you had the outhouse re-dug, a two seater
so it'd last longer, you won't need to do it again.
You are weighing up whether the jetty will need work
or if, in its already haphazard state, it may last you.

And now you're holding your head out of water
not because you don't know the dip and glide of a good stroke
but for safety's sake, so the sudden motor boats
which ferry up weekenders and supplies
will see you, here where they don't expect you,
so far out from the land.

Adam Horovitz

Water, Prayer

Water, pure in its cradle-glass,
is trembling sea in miniature, where lips
beach the meniscus and then gently pass
it back; a constant recycling of sips.

Each mouthful is a moving on, a cloud
as deeply housed as dreams of rain.
In paddling pool, in tap, in cup it's flowed
from *it* to *us*, and there, and back again.

It's in the engine of this world, the flow;
water, the roaring constancy of change.
It plumps the hidden seed and makes it grow
and can, with time, bring down a mountain range.

It is itself a prayer. Hold out your hand.
Watch water rub fear down to grains of sand.

Martin Jackson

Saatchi: compositions in Black and Red no. 1

On Ecopoiesis

Research told us about
the Basics of Adulthood.
Tri-decade transitioning
is something hard to conceive
as childhood dreams are dashed.
We are not special.

Achieving autonomy
is not linear, as hoped,
but soft drinks are well placed
to deliver moments
of self-actualisation.
That hoped for better you.

We called the solution
Grown-up Innocence
and proved it using
a two-minute mood film
(Home Alone, Trigger Happy,
Shrek's donkey snorting cocaine)

followed by storyboards.
We explained that the fridge
would have only eggs, milk, juice,
and that it would be more 'fridge'
than the fridge in the drawings.
(Smeg, without being Smeg).

There were rushes and rough cuts
and we elevated the dramatic tone.
Early CGI was circulated
against our strict wishes.
There was a meeting to explain
why we had to be trusted.

Weekly WiP meet-ups
became daily FTP downloads
as the sigh at the start
was made to suggest:
'I want nothing more
than to go there.'

The one towards the end:
'I'm thankful for having
avoided so many deaths.'
We were too far down
the line to zoom into
the personality of the fruit.

A timeframe was constructed
around David Bellamy.
Concerns his delivery
lacked clarity dissipated
as less words became
more powerful. More filmic.

The packshot was pearlised.
The splat icon took weeks
to be satisfactorily rendered.
There were sunbursts, lens flare.
Fingers of god were made punchier.
They were brand properties.

Samantha Jackson

Resurrection

Inside the lip and curl of coarse
and pleated skin, jellied rose-gold flesh
suspends a spray of amber pips;
life is bedded here, held in sugared stasis.

Like a sea-chest hauled to land, rusted
from too much time in salty deeps,
it has been beaten by the sun;
a slub of stalk hunches from the ain

It's as if the fruit has come full circle,
gone back to seed, its shrunken body
a kernel of itself: I want to plant it,
grow it again, for its frail shape to

soften, swell, unfurl like a new petal,
spread roots like giant wings
in the soil, fly up again
through the earth.

Heidi James

Dungeness Lighthouse

Climbing up in a spiral
as if crawling through
a snail shell
towards the old light
the lens pink and orange
latticed by lead
like the apple pies
baked by Auntie George
when we were small
her thick wrists
circled by silver bangles
and the scar where they
cut off
her wedding ring
her finger outgrowing the gold loop

At the top we look out over the shale
huts collapsing plank by plank
the sea further now
held back by increasing banks
of pebbles
time accumulating land mass
you say, 'Let's stay up here, let's never go back down.'
But we do, carefully,
step by step.

Sarah James

The Farmhouse Kitchen

Grandma's green Aga stove lid is raised like a giant bed warmer,
smells of bacon and crushed cornflake cakes with cheese reaching over
to us children at the big, thick wooden table where we're hungry,
always hungry, always excited, never still, waiting for
the clunk of those breakfast cups, bowls, plates of cream ringed with
    blue,
yellow breaking from egg yolks, butter oozing from toast to fingers,
that licked curl of them through my hair, laughing
and shouting and pulling my brother's hair as he tugs at my arm
and all that time my small, tired, rigid-as-a-bowling-pin Grandma
smiling,
    while the big, big milk jug squats in the centre of the table
                                 and Grandad's
glasses scan the paper, silent, almost unmoving, except for that slight
    twist
of wrist and fingers to turn the pages, a rustle, rustle, then scratch
of his crossword pen until he finally looks up, chuckles, eyes jigging
as he picks up the big blue-ringed milk jug and lifts its creamy contents
    to him,
always full to brimming, never spilling.

Andrew Jamison

Listening to Kings of Convenience

In the arpeggioed, folky early stuff
like Toxic Girl, the bass drum's dumph-dumph-dumph

which signals the lead solo, stands out a mile,
the timing of it almost as comical

as the dink-dink-dink of the opening harmonic –
somewhere between idyllic and ironic –

and the bassline saunters, bum-bums along,
like all good basslines, only noticed when it's gone.

Anna Johnson

Diner

I've seen no golden bridges or Berkeley lawns.
No galleries or Beat-lit seedy-alley haunts.

Instead, in downtown dives, on acetate black
tabletops deeply etched with other's hours

I scribble down the passing people days. I watch
beside the plate-glass window-world

as otherwisely constellated lives negotiate
the rain, time, I don't yet recognise.

I draw the city. And myself inside it, drinking tea,
waiting for the time to leave my pen and go find the sea.

Evan Jones

Cavafy in Liverpool

Here is your sad young man:
he is ship-to-shore, he is buttoned-down
in tweed and scarved, eyes closed
when the Mersey wind

calls his collar to his ear
on the strand near Albert Dock,
some January, some winter day
we recognise but take no part in.

Here is your boy at the end of the shore
while the waters continue
touching place and nothing,
hold something dear and don't,

the desire and devotion
to an island he never dreams.
Not summoned, not answered,
he searches the world growing dim

as the river swells and recedes,
like closed eyelids shifting during sleep.
One less wave, he thinks, one less,
and then the Persians can get through.

Francesca Jones

Heron

You were watching our garden painted
with snow, from the window;
you worried about the fish under all that ice,
when the heron landed.

Usually you'd scare him away,
bang a saucepan with a wooden spoon,
an erratic warning rhythm
defending your ornamental carp;
but today you stopped.
The fish were trapped,
the heron hungry,
and you, you were tired
with the monotony.

Joshua Jones

Home

Flung as if waking from a dream: the city appears and heaves
a catalogue of memories from the train. The disclosure of its neon
burns like the pages as they fall. You see this passing over a bridge
where the water is so black it could equally be
a bottomless drop. When the window's dark mirror shuts the city out
your homelessness returns, now with no recollections
to pad the sides. The tannoy announces the imminent arrival
of your destination. Your face is pale and hot as the speed buckles,
        heart
kicking, confused, caged, or not, but moving, blind, and sore
        with hunger.

Meirion Jordan

Iarlles y Ffynawn

In the bright frame of a girl's dress
time stops. A breeze rustles the gauze
which might be a sleeve, or skirts.

Beyond, the landscape is very small.
Owein in his tiny, archaic clothes
– scarlets and greens – runs over the grass

and beyond the high wall of the garden
a few towers stretch into a blue heaven,
their flags hardly lifting in the light airs.

And that is all. A dog barks and falls silent.
The girl's dress moves careless as brushwork
and the man runs – but from what, and to what?

Mike Kavanagh

The Boys of Billy Joel Crescent, 1986

tormented the alcoholic millionaire on the corner
threw rocks from cliffs to hurt a boy in the river
skinny-dipped in neighbour's pools after dark
followed rusty tracks out past the feed mill
hid from Old Curry's ghost in the woods
ran naked in the valley on hot nights
tied a kid to a tree and left him
threw apples at the bus driver
started fires in their yards
pissed on each other
kicked pumpkins
skipped school
skateboarded
f-worded
scrapped
smoked
drifted

Luke Kennard

Some Svengali *You* Turned Out To Be
The last permutational prose poem I will ever write

We were applauded just for being alive. The adult attempts to saw the
world in half. The child obeys him.

We were applauded for our 'fallen into a toybox' look. The adult
attempts to justify the harshest cruelties and egotism of his
friend through a sincere examination of his own conscience. The
child pushes him into a shark tank.

We were applauded for our no nonsense take on the infantilism of our
generation. The adult is left blank for your own message. The
child is *SORRY YOU'RE LEAVING.*

We were applauded for our delicious stuffing mix. The adult cannot
   remember for the life of him why he went downstairs and has
   gone upstairs to jog his memory – or was he downstairs in the
   first place and must go back there to jog his memory about why
   he is now upstairs? The child has remained stationary
   throughout and is wearing your spectacles.

We were applauded for not taking you too seriously when you said
   our whole practice was built on bogus foundations. The adult
   just said his first sincere thing today at twenty minutes past
   three. The child will be right with you after he finishes reading
   comment number 16 under an Amazon review of a novel he
   hasn't read, but suspects has been poorly served by its amateur
   critics; 'To what tributary,' he mutters, 'to what run-off pool have
   I channelled my thoughts?'

We were applauded for our bogus foundations. The adult snaps a
   chocolate bar in half and admires an edifice. The child kicks over
   a city.

We were applauded for self-loathing and self-publishing. The adult's
   favourite question is 'Any thoughts?' The child's raised eyebrow
   is more than sufficient.

We were applauded for diminishing returns and doing the washing
   up. The adult takes work where it can find it. The child carries
   all your furniture downstairs, piece by piece.

We were applauded for the inherent limitations of our craft. The adult
   was killed in an explosion. The child is skilled at exposition.

We were applauded for endless repetition. The adult attempts to
   compose herself, the child outruns its own programme.

Amy Key

Interiorana

Ornaments spy on my quilt, its down
frayed where toes catch the tender

edge. The window rattles discontent.
Outside many tongues are flush

against their roofs, seeking an iced unison.
And in this room: flowers go to paper

as they sink down their measure;
an origami of ideas; socks steam

gently under the window; the draught
alerts my skin. To court day

I taste mineral-lush condensation,
unfrost the view, scent the room

with butter-sweetened pastries.
Over years, I'll acquire a chandelier

of silver spoons – each a different size –
some pewtered with age. When cold comes

they'll shiver high, bright tones.
Inside I fritter soft as cinders.

Katharine Kilalea

Kolya's Nails

All night, the quiet countryside was ruined by the sound of Kolya's
     nails
to-ing and fro-ing from her water bowl on the melamine floor.

You're much too sensitive, said Jo, I slept like a log.
And so what? There's more comfort in a dog than sleep.

Early the next morning we went walking, just Kolya and I.
I walked slowly as though the air was thick.

I opened a stile at the fence and Kolya wriggled through
and ran ahead, scattering cows, gobbled up

almost immediately by the long, dewy grass, the mist.
If there was a short cut, it was not the route she discovered

but what came over me in her absence. I saw it in the cows,
how they came down to the fence where I was standing

– confused and crying for her in the howling way
we call to dogs – and stared. They looked at me

with their caviar eyes and chewed sideways,
as though I were something spectacular,

or something that didn't add up. She would come back,
the fool, she always did, like a springy branch.

Simon King

Transonic Acceleration

If I were up there – not the pilot but
the plane, a solid fuselage with wings
to cut the air and lift me up above
this town, rising on a corkscrew white smoke
tail – I'd carry you away from this field
at fifty metres per second towards
a ceiling thirteen thousand metres off
the ground, through cloud cover where we could lose
all referential, all sight and just be
pilot you and airplane me. One compressed
transonic blur. Weightless for a moment
and free of the world, before falling back,

tumbling, air break disengaged. Pulling up
in our final moments, tearing away.

Caleb Klaces

Plastic holy

I used to believe that families lived inside the Berlin Wall,
          which I assumed to be as thick as my house
and hollowed out like a baguette. Nobody noticed
          until I had eaten the evidence.
But where would the rubble have gone? O where
          does it ever go? Space seems to have
plenty of space. But it is a kind of idea, out there.
          Here, things are so heartbreakingly material.
On the steps of the vast Blue Mosque
          someone hands out little blue plastic bags to snap
over visitors' shoes. That the means we have of being holy
          crackles on the soft carpet
like a baby's nappy. That the money for the funeral
          comes from a loud day of playing cards
in the same cemetery where everyone lives.
          The girl who sleeps between corrugated iron
and cloth on graves stacked three high is glad
          of the bodies. Up there, it is easier to breathe,
a little further from the plastic bags and plastic bags
          of shit. That the waste products
of holiness end up where people live and die
          and are holy. With my clean-air, clean-
conscience fortune, I took her out on a sled. Marie,
          I said, Marie, this is snow, this is falling
for fun.

Richard Lambert

The Magnolia

Will you watch the wind blow
white blossom from the tree,
will you watch it blow,

the branches strained with love,
the garden stained with white,
will you watch the wind?

A blackbird leaps into the height
and sings; sky is blue.
Will you watch it blow?

The whiteness is a gift.
Soft, and slow, it opens
on the limbs. Watch it so.

Agnes Lehoczky

November meals on wheels

An atypical ringtone. Your falling cadences. The family is well;
quiet but not surprised. She was found in the kitchen two days
after your last visit, lying on the floor in her patterned gown,
her dinner can hanging on the door since Monday, unattended.

You are there; I am here, and this here and there is so well-defined
that no metaphysics can fuse them into one world yet you want
identical autumn, identical time zone identical region of the earth;
that hour matters. It is everything. All our belongings are in that hour
dissected in three-thousand and six hundred seconds.

That hour is in-between. There's no overlap but in the solar time
in that interval between two successive returns of the sun.
I too have been preparing for a cycle ride for years. Planning a route
back to the meridian, round an imaginary circle. Watching the
     satellite
for snow. Muffling all footpaths. Snowing up windscreens of maps.

I am sorry to hear your grandmother's dead. Have you thought
of those happenings in-between? She may have tripped. Hit her head.
Have you thought of that suspicious distance? That arc faded between
the upright and the floor tiles. Two days' secret of her life. Let it be.
No, there is no sign of intrusion, nothing's been taken; the flat stands
     the same.

Frances Leviston

Propylaea

It is properly
the gate before the gate,
the entrance before the entrance,
a huge tautology

made of marble
and the old ambition
to be understood in a certain way.
The long approach

up hairpin
rubble resembling steps
towards the massive entablature
and baking summit

frames blue sky
and the heads of those
who comprehend in the foreground;
it glorifies

more than ever
the sanctuaries waiting
beyond, behind these colonnades'
unprotected sides.

When there is
an opening but no dividing
wall, the emphasis falls on process
instead of destination –

that is to say,
you come with your hands
shielding your eyes, in deference,
or not at all;

and those of us
who make the passage
correctly cannot return by the same
route that shut

its eye invisibly
after we entered, and hope
for the opposite change in reverse:
we are stuck

in the kingdom
of knowledge we came
here for, too perfectly primed
inductees of a cult

finding what
they thought was true
more true when it finally occurs,
forms emerging

as the dust clears,
enormous structures
maintaining their perspectives
from the deep past

to here. It has
all been done before:
original figures, the seven plots.
We can relax

beside the stone-
sandalled caryatids,
their unmoved skirts giving shade
from the sun

as it's shone
for thousands of years,
lighting all this toil and splendour;
can feel our own

ambitions recede
then colossally resurge,
partial and imposing, like the door
behind the door,

hinged on nothing,
promising this: *if there is*
an opening but no dividing wall,
the emphasis falls…

Joanne Limburg

Welcome to the United States

Halfway to the home of the deceased,
I met a man with the softest voice in all Chicago

and offered him my passport (which,
to give some form to agony, I had almost bitten through).

He took it, and my mother's, apologised so sweetly
for the queue that I forgave him (but not America)

for being what he was. He had brown eyes,
and when he asked the purpose of our visit

and I explained, I thought they brimmed a bit,
like mine were brimming. I felt us

brim together, the soft-voiced man and I;
we were both of us bewildered, and so sorry

and we had to wonder, both of us, why someone
with a family would do a thing like that. *His* brother –

– well not quite the same but in a way – missing for a month, a junkie,
they found him when they dragged the lake –

so I was sorry now for his loss too, we were both
so sorry, and brimming together, and his fingers

were so deft and elegant as they tapped the keys, and how
warm, how tender his feeling heart under his uniform

as shyly, willingly, I ceded him my fingertips,
and offered up my eyes, and believe me, in that moment,

he could have taken everything, that soft-voiced man,
just to give some form to agony, that we might brim together.

Fran Lock

Year of the Rabbit

I understand
the temptation.

You saw the sob run
the length of my arm
like the recoil from a gun.

You saw the promiscuous
pinks of my eyes,
the colour of raw meat
like the lurid weepers of widows.

And you said: weak.

You saw the lowercase curve of my spine,
my ankles like cufflinks, my titbit
nakedness, shaking
like fanned-flames.

You saw me, sexed me, my nuptial bud,
split like the grooved hoof of an orchid.

You saw the slow spooling
of whorehair, yellow-blonde,
small pulse like the drip
of a leaky tap.

And you said: weak. I understand.

You weren't to know
how my ovaries waxed
electrical,

my small body thrum-happy,
a vexing battery.

You weren't to know
that my quickness isn't shy
but skilled,

that to me they built temples
so my heart would keep
their confessions
like an apple keeps maggots.

I am lithe, a live-wire, alive.

And this year
we celebrate
the rabbit.

Kim Lockwood

The Curve

Bed's comfy enough at my back,
arm in lax fifth position, toes curled.

Hands cold, tentative, around the curve,
on the play of bone between the breasts.

The touch is touch, to calm, to quiet.

And I miss that cowardice under the covers
I laughed through before,

when this was pleasure,
yesterday, and not this Monday afternoon

when the locum stares ahead
in politesse and says,

yes, there's a lump
under there, and I have to nod and try

not to shy away from composure
as she talks of referrals and scans,

then pauses, searching for how to say don't worry
in ways that will make it work.

I miss when it was you, when we didn't know,
in our world of Sunday morning,

when touch was calm, slow, quiet.

Mike Loveday

Fool's Errand

Beyond the requests –
issued my first day at his factory –
for striped paint, or a ham salad doughnut,
it's the glass hammer and rubber nails
which come to mind now, as I'm fixing
his image into this.

Hannah Lowe

Fist

When my brother put his fist through a window
on New Year's Eve, no one noticed until a cold draft
cooled our bodies dancing. There was rainbow light
from a disco ball, silver tinsel round the pictures.
My brother held his arm out to us, palm
upturned, a foot high spray of blood.
This was Ilford, Essex, 1993, nearly midnight,
us all smashed on booze and Ecstasy and Billy,
6 foot 5, folding at the knee, a shiny fin of glass
wedged in his wrist. We walked him to
the kitchen, the good arm slung on someone's neck,
Gary shouting *Billy*, Darren phoning for
an ambulance, the blood was everywhere. I pressed
a towel across the wound, around
the glass and led him by the hand into the
garden, he stumbled down into the snow,
slurring *leave it out* and *I'm ok*. A girl was crying in
the doorway, the music carried on, the bass line
thumping as we stood around my brother, Gary talking
gently saying *easy fella*, Darren draining Stella in one
hand and in the other, holding up my brother's arm,
wet and red, the veins stood out like branches. I thought
that he was dying, out there in the snow and I
got down, I knelt there on the ice

and held my brother, who I never touched, and never told
I loved, and even then I couldn't say it
so I listened to the incantation *easy fella*
and my brother's breathing,
felt him rolling forward, all that weight, Darren
throwing down his can and yelling *Billy, don't you dare*
and shaking him. My brother's face was grey,
his lips were loose and pale and I
was praying. Somewhere in the street, there was
a siren, there was a girl inside who blamed
herself, there were men with blankets
and a tourniquet, they stopped my brother bleeding,
as the New Year turned, they saved him,
the snow was falling hard, they saved us all.

Alex MacDonald

Family Tree

Under the mown lawns rest the elders.
Heads shot with tongues, long since dissolved,
And hands bound with rest,
Are our deliveries to the earth.

Further below rest their ancestors,
Faces battered with age, knees knocked
Against an oak case, throats melted away,
The vocal cords tightened like artichoke hearts.

Further and further we dig.
Searching for something familiar, we dig up roots,
And hold relics up to one another,
Offering them to the sun.

Sophie Mackintosh

Third Person

This is the only thing I love more than you;
the third person standing at the foot of the bed,
watching us sleep the whole night through.

Close all the doors. Sprinkle yarrow and rue,
a home-made exorcism, hands on my forehead
as I think of the only thing I love more than you.

I tell you of my dreams. You wrack them for clues
as in cards or tea-leaves begging to be read,
then we sleep again, are watched the whole night through.

In one febrile dream I dreamt that I grew
out of this paper room, back to life instead,
a place with nothing loved more than you

(which is what you deserve, I know you do –
not the possessed girl, refusing to be fed,
watched through fractured sleep the whole night through) –

you quieten me, whisper predictions for us two
beyond this time of fumes and fast, vinegar and lead,
past the only thing that I love more than you,
that still watches, watches us, the whole night through.

Kathryn Maris

Darling, Would You Please Pick Up Those Books?

How many times do I have to say
get rid of the books off the goddamn floor
do you have any idea how it feels
to step over books you wrote about *her*
bloody hell you sadist what kind of man
are you all day long those fucking books

in my way for 3 years your *acclaimed* books
tell me now what do you have to say
for yourself you think you're such a man
silent brooding pondering at the floor
pretending you're bored when I mention *her*
fine change the subject ask 'Do I feel

like I need more medication' NO I don't *feel
like I need more medication* it's the books
don't you see don't you see it's *her*
why don't you listen to anything I say
and for god's sake books on the floor
are a *safety hazard* remember that man

from Cork who nearly died fine that man
fell over a hurley not a book but I don't feel
you're getting the point the point is that a floor
is not an intelligent place for books
books *I* have to see and books that say
exactly where and how you shagged her

what shirt she wore before you shagged her
I can write a book too about some man
better still about *you* I can say
something to *demonize* you how would you feel
about *that* ha ha why don't I write a book
about how I *hoover your sodding floor*

and how you've *never once* hoovered your floor
why can't I be a muse why can't I be a 'her'
what does one have to do to be in a book
around here do I have to be *dead* for a man
to write me a poem how do you think it feels
to be non muse material can't you say

you feel for me what you felt for her
can't you say I'm better than that woman
can't you get those books off the floor?

Timothy Marthur

The Deadly Sins – No. 1 Lust

The night I tried to French kiss my father it wasn't entirely unexpected. We'd been watching *Dynasty* where women opened the doors to their apartments wearing nothing but a bath towel and then kissed the man standing there open mouthed. My father and I were members of the opposite sex I'd reasoned. After nine years of the same old goodnight kiss on the lips he might appreciate some variation.

I'd lent in over the wing of his armchair with my jaw slightly ajar. He'd laughed. Then I got an explanation. Did he say that that type of kissing was for girlfriends and boyfriends? Husbands and wives? That that was the way they kissed in France?

The humiliation was no worse than the time I'd lifted my hands for bread, aged five, at the Communion Table. And while I still wasn't aspiring to join the Church of England, I was sure I'd grow up to be a millionaire's daughter, up in my penthouse, man's tongue in my mouth, bath towel sliding towards the floor.

Sophie Mayer

Today is the day of the smashing of dishes

Today is the day of the smashing of dishes.
Clothes left to rot on the vine.
Today we gather the work of our hands.
Let it crash, let it salt the floor of heaven
in its non-existence. What's heaven
to such things – rain, overdrafts, dishes, spiders,
the elongated leg
of panic shadowing at you out of
corners as you write, as you pretend to
write by leaving
comments on friends' posts, friend being
a word as
elastic as money
or war or
heaven, and as meaningless –
What indeed. It's a blister popped to reveal
blue sky, a revenant, a rhyme
word not un-useful, a flat cloth
covering loss of heart (or for doffing at the past). What's
heaven when it swings, when the cares
that hung around you through the week seem
to vanish. What's lost then, in
its vast, slappable face, its flaunted cloak
of crushed turquoise
worn with pie-eyed innocence: no more
than a scrap, a colloidal illusion, a colossal insult
tossed at you with that arrogant head-toss
only oaks can manage. Burn them down.
I mean really: Nature? Will it wash the dishes, or dry them? Wash
the clothes or dry them?
Only atmospherically. Only
metaphorically does it
resound with what slips
from our slippery hands.

Chris McCabe

Mark E. Smith

The man on the Todmorden tram doesn't know who he is
– gurning power-loofah of his jaws –
he could have come straight from the docks
in an oversized suit, mucky fingers sniffling
elephantine sleeves. At the bar the Stanley flame
of his self-belief cuts & singes a leaf in bunsen blue,
distinctly not a worker – *just a well-read punk peasant* –
keeps his secrets like a travel-pack of biscuits in his breast
pocket, never indelibly writes down his own words
but keeps them as kids locked-out on the latch,
unpackaging one line into five with the potcheen of chiasmus.
Under a Salford sink he once shrouded his sisters
with an off-white sheet to position them as Japanese
Prisoners of War – when he got to eighteen the only
way to continue the game was to make a band *depend*
on his lyrics for success. So plays the macabre uncle
cutting his nephew's first Giro into strips, or the Family
Business Father who cursed his children at home & at work.
The bassist stares down on the floor when he comes near
then looks lost & bereft when he goes past – fade-out
stage right to reappear stage-left five minutes later –
a (near-religious) resonance (some said) in his presence
of straight-cut jeans & ox-musk leather coat,
the only NO being to spend time with other artists,
musicians, writers – poseurs of no crap experience –
so when Morrissey newly famous ducked into the Green
Room like a stand-in geography teacher his confidence
groaned in regret at the memory of the fan-mail he'd sent
– 'I've still got all those letters Steven' – staring still gurning
the power-loofah of his jowels that locks resilient lexicon out
on the latch – how can you regret *anything* that's ever said?
A palette of false teeth wedged into a journalist's neck
another man who lives off his words but doesn't think
(though since some nervous hacks found him rather *nice*)
– pleasant & courteous even – before fading off under
the dreadnought afternoon cloud of Manchester Town
for Deutsch beer – anonymous as such a face allows –

collecting pieces of vernacular like lounge-bar moths,
democratically allowing the workers to stand their drinks
then jawing jar-for-jar with the man – any man – through
the licensed door just off the tram from Todmorden.

Richie McCaffrey

Spinning Plates

My mother was mad as mercury,
mad as a silken Disraeli stovepipe
hat hiding a gypsum-white rabbit.

She once told me, the malt talking,
that I wasn't her first born boy,
there had been seminal drafts.

She said that being pregnant
was like spinning a bone-china plate
on the thinnest stick inside you.

Breakages were bound to occur.
It was a question of which piece
could drop intact and roll around

on a hardwood floor, its rim ringing
with cries. My sister is an artisan
firing, a wild coloured plate

still atwirl. I am a white canteen
saucer, ready to be tanned with tea-
slops. A cupped palm for spillages.

John McCullough

Night Writing

In humid months, at the estate's unwatched edge,
the boys gather for an after-hours cigarette

before trashing field gates. All boast Reeboks, earrings,
their honed geezer-laughs rev-revving

with the engines of graffiti-tagged bangers.
Customized stereos thump out speed garage,

the race kicking off in a blizzard of chalk dust,
their bouncing charge towards a crooked iron post.

Death and dew ponds can't stop them while they swerve
past quivering teasel, conquer the bone ridge's turn,

skeins of wool lifting from gorse as banners
for the night's whooping, fist-raising winners.

Further off, the crews unite for a slow drift, melt into hills
but leave the empty sky with headlamp trails:

blazing ghosts still performing their necessary work,
still scribbling their names on the dark.

Michelle McGrane

Princesse de Lamballe

He skewers my matted, blonde head on a pike,
shows me the city's less-fêted sights:
growling alleys and ravenous back streets
guttered with urine, nightsoil and vermin;
toothless, frayed women queuing for bread,
each coarse, weevilled loaf fourteen copper *sous*;
the Hôpital des Quinze-Vingt's shuffling inmates
tapping for alms amid the stalls of Les Halles;
Saint-Marcel tanneries' frame-stretched hides
kneaded supple with beef greaves and brains;
the Seine choked with debris and tangled milfoil,
a carcass sliding into the Pont Neuf's shadows.

The Queen's playing *tric-trac* in the tower,
twenty guards flanking the Temple's iron portal.
She's raised the stakes, the bone dice clattering
across the pearwood and ebony board.
The scrofulous *sans-culotte* belting *Ça Ira*
braces my face to the crosshatched casing,
my fractured cheek arch, bloodied tongue,
smashed teeth, splintered jaw.
Remember Petit Trianon, ma chérie,
the dovecote and mill, cherry orchard and lake.
Remember the hyacinths we planted last autumn,
how we split our sides milking the goats.

Michael McKimm

The Ice Harvest

At that time of the year the river froze
and the men entered my life, young and old,
men who thought no difference between
felling timber and sawing blocks from ice,
who carried hats in their hands before
my mother, and had snow in their beards,

110

huge furls of snow that came with them
from Iowa, Illinois: wind-harried, twisted
ghosts, laying down on the ice, day after day.
I brought them soup, eggs when we had them.
When their fingers blued or bled I used
warm water, salts, tried to eke a smile
from their sunken eyes, and if there was
a fiddle night I'd dance short silly jigs.
Each afternoon I went out with their lunch
on a woven sled. The ice creaked under
the weight of men but did not budge, seemed
to like the stress and heave, the give
and the not give, its interminable strength:
Look what I have done to your great river.
Stopped it in its tracks. I went from man
to man with bread and coffee, watched them
guide the horses on the grids, the one-armed
saws going in, picks nudging loose blocks
into the channel. They laughed at me
shivering. *That'll shrink your balls.* Boys
not much older than me had sawdust
in their hair and on their undershirts
when they returned from the ice house. It fell
like quavers of snow to the kitchen floor.
They taught me cards, forbidden games.
I did not tell them of the part I'd play
in the coming months, when they were gone,
when ice that was not loaded onto trains
was hauled around the summer streets,
sold to cool the drinks in the big hotel.
I did not tell them this, or other things,
just pretended all was dory when the trees
began to drip and we welcomed in the thaw.

Alex McRae

Chimney Sweep

Drum-tight inside the flue, the sweep
explores the other side of walls in greyish points of lace.
After years in darkness, he's begun to seep
and bloom in damp roses swirled above the fireplace.

A dainty Chinese empress bricked into the walls
sanctifies this house, a box within a box. Nevertheless,
cats won't enter this room. Nothing falls
down the blocked shaft. He listens, motionless.

His back is bunched, the way a whippet draws
her haunches in before a surge. Each fused foot
forms a whorled spine in miniature. Between floors
this small mollusc nests in birdlime and soot.

Halfway to heaven, he is light as a blown egg;
a bell snug in its steeple, a round hole with a round peg.

Isabella Mead

The False Floor

Beneath the floor of the Old Operating Theatre
and the ceiling of St Thomas' Church
where heaven and earth are inverted,
a three-inch space is stuffed with sawdust,
a horsehair filament between science and religion
to stifle the screams and mute the blood.
And it begins now, a steady ruby blush
dyeing the mousebrown splinters into starkness
and welling to a point of saturation
just at the tip of each splinter, no more;
so the church below continues
pure unblemished prayer.

Emily Middleton

I start with the principle and passion of organisms

I start with the principle and passion
of organisms. I pour iron ore and coke
through the head of a leopard
rescued from the workshop
of a taxidermist.

Next, I add the limestone, crumbled
like cake mixture with the legs of arachnids
to the blues of Ray Charles. This is lonely work.

It's soon time for the saprotrophs.
They sit and soak
like carnivorous lily pads.
At the back of the chamber
saplings quiver, battling all the while
to photosynthesise. I smoke
and sit for twenty-eight evenings,
waiting till the moon is out and watching it fatten,
gorging on the night till it slides
out of sight, outlived again by the stars.

I use the tap I made myself, long ago
in metalwork class, its spout shaped
like a serpent's mouth (the theme was gothic).
It's old now and flaking rust like dead skin,
but it suits my purpose. I twist,
and the slag slugs out.

The furnace is finally ready,
whistling fitfully and sweating black gases.
I've lost my mask, but no matter;
I've survived too many times.

The crescendo is coming, I can hear
the tinny clanging of metallic hooves –
twenty-two seconds then they charge
army-strong out of the predator's head

in an instant trepanning: my horsemen,
shining in the shroud of steam, dripping
carbon like bombs, cells quivering
in the invisible slipstream,
iron-clad wheels shrieking
on highways
only they can know.

James Midgley

Phineas survives

but all the clouds are anvils on his back.
On my back – is it my back? I lean away
from my hands as if they are lizards.
Always those brown little lizards
would sun themselves in the parched air
by the tracks. Phineas summons rain
now, and here it pours. Its metal rounds
are one and a quarter inches in diameter.
Phineas drops to his knees and I reach
to pull him from the dirt,
a bridge leant down to drink its river,
but the lizards are under the hot sun and here
is the hot sun. We are a centre.
Thunder overhead, underhead, in the head.
Phin, you've dropped your hammer.
I move to scoop it from the ground
but it figures my nails wrong and thuds.
Nothing hurts. Sneezing
hurts, sometimes. I will find myself
scattered in the grass near a pair of boots,
sitting on a sleeper, inside the fireplace
that keeps the engine hurtling.
Small thoughts, you can come
out of hiding now. Goddamn it, Phin, goddamn.
And that too: Phineas has been god,
genius of a leaking faucet. To be expected.
In one of my memories I am looking at a skull
in a museum. In another I am a black eel
made of metal, ready to be thrown.
Phin, I say, Phin, come out of the tunnel, but
I cannot: speak or come out of the tunnel.
Some archer has drawn back my spine.

Phineas P. Gage (1823 – 1860) was a railroad construction foreman who survived an accident which drove an iron rod through his head, The injury is reported to have changed his personality so friends saw him as 'no longer Gage'.

Stefan Mohamed

Kitchen

All the saucepans have been stolen.
I'll use that helmet of yours. The one from the war.
Except it's got bullet holes in it.

So maybe I just won't cook. I'll have something cold.
Except there's no ice left in the freezer.
We used it all up in mojitos.
Can't even have one of them now.
The cold left the fridge because we weren't paying it enough.
It's floating around in the atmosphere somewhere. Waiting.

I could have something from the cupboard.
A biscuit? No. The biscuit tin melted and the biscuits vaporized.
I can't remember why.

Mice ruined all the other stuff, like mustard, which I don't like anyway,
and Marmite and peanut butter. Which I do.
And you used up all the herbs and spices making a collage (it's a
        lovely collage, to be fair).

I'd have a cup of tea, but the kettle's broken. That's my fault.
I have a short fuse so I borrowed one from the kettle.
There's been no tea or coffee for weeks, but at least I haven't lost my
        temper.

You might lose yours, though.
Maybe we'll just eat out tonight.

Kim Moore

The Dream

I dreamt of a man who slept like a bear.
My husband awoke, so I dropped
to the floor, played dead for hours.

I dreamt of a man who howled like a wolf.
My husband crept in with a hang-dog look,
brought love-bites, apologies, flowers.

I dreamt of a man who was slow as a snake.
In the morning my husband was wrapped
round my neck, and tightening, tightening.

I dreamt of a man who sang like a bird.
When I awoke the trees had been felled
and my husband had murdered the garden.

Helen Mort

Thinspiration Shots

i
Beneath the site's italics – *if you eat
you'll never dance again* – a close up
of a ballerina, veins like wires,
balancing on a single satin shoe.

You dreamt of being small enough
to fit inside your grandma's jewellery box:
the dancer spinning on her gold left leg,
a mirror doubling her, the tinny music playing

on and on until the lid was shut at last,
and she was tiny, locked in with the dark.

ii

You've seen this photograph before: the pout,
the offered playing card, top hat that weighs
as much as her, the plume of hair curled
round her neck, wrists slender as a wand.

You think about the things she's hiding
up her sleeve: the queen, the ace
or last night's dinner in a paper bag.
And yes, you know her tricks by heart:

the one with all the handkerchiefs, the one
where she makes herself disappear.

iii

One model has a waist just like a snake.
The other is all whippet ribs, her legs
are slender as a deer's. The way she
rests one hand against the fence

light as a hummingbird, as if she's never still
reminds you of those hours of press ups
when the lights were out,
the dizzy sit ups before dawn

the miles you ran away from home,
near fainting, trying to give yourself the slip.

iv

Scroll down. A brunette in a mermaid pose
almost too light to break the surface of the lake.
You would have drunk its contents if you could,
those days they put you on the scales,

your bladder swollen as a gourd.
When they were sure they had
enough of you, you'd go upstairs
and lock the bathroom door,

you'd crouch above the cool white bowl
and piss it all away.

v

Across this picture of a convex stomach,
someone's added 'Intake', text in bold:
B – glass of water. L – a slice of bread.
D – nothing. Guys, my willpower sucks.

You think about the friends who slimmed
to paperbacks, so thin they'd slip
between your shelves, the condensed
chapters of their limbs, the narrative

of barely-hidden bones. The ending
promised from the start.

vi

Once, you might have taken them for wings:
the shoulder blades jutting from the blonde
who stands on a hill, her naked back
to the camera. The shape of her

is surely made for flight, but these days
now your mirror's not a magnifying glass,
you see the ground waiting beneath the sky,
the skull waiting beneath the skin,

a girl no stronger than a wingless bird,
a wind that wouldn't lift her if it could.

Beverley Nadin

S11

I tell you, this was real.
With my sharpened pencil, down Sharrow Vale,
I set out to track the zeitgeist, or the gist,
for a full colour feature.
Word on the street – World Cup twenty-ten?
Eurovision? Recession. No. I'd need an angle
specific, local: an audit
on Arctic Monkeys cover groups;
the preference for 'snicket'
over 'ginnel'
in S11 as against S2.

I sidestepped for a maple pecan slice
and a quick poll with the hostess
re: sales of edible luxury goods,
disposable incomes. Her accomplice, Mick,
tossed his pennyworth in
on the cost of living and breathing.
He had the hump
with the NHS. As I chalked up bullet points,
one of their flashing chariots
dropped at speed through the valley.
It pulled up across the street at *Velours, Valerie.*

Before I could turn a leaf in my spiral jotter
they were in and out with a stretcher,
spouting off about ventricles,
valves, pulmonary lingo
I made a note to Google. Something like broccoli:
bronchi, bronchiectasis. Broad stains
darkened their standard-issue greens.
There was more to this than bronchitis.
Somebody went feet-first
on a magic carpet ride
to the back of the van, workboots side by side.

I found out later he was dead as a brontosaurus.
The ballpoint behind his ear
is the last I remember.

Welcome to the Emporium
of Dinge sniggered a door hinge. In the dim shop
I lifted a velvet drape the colour of Dijon
and the darkness
drew back, revealing
driftwood of trilbies,
buttons, chess sets, walnut
holders for cigarettes, etc. I ad-libbed
a nose for vintage bric-à-brac
as a matter of technique,
sizing up a teapot shaped like Battenberg.
Somebody sneezed. I tripped on a beanbag.

I couldn't shake the feeling I'd seen him before.
He was under eighteen;
according to girth, under-eating.
He mined a stack of vinyl with a road drill's
concentration
for a glint of bootleg or limited edition.
A rough snort sketched a web of phlegm.
This was no caffeine thrill: he'd line up a dose
to rival the trouser leg
of his Adidas.
I managed a sound like *hello* that came out
hollow, like a smoke ring. When he said
'I bet you look good on the dance floor'
I considered leaving.

The voice was familiar. Alex Turner?
I scanned for exits. He blocked the rear.
He sleeved a forty-five.
I found my groove – of course! It was Rolex Tanner,
frontman of the Arctic Funkies, or was it
the Hectic Junkies?
I took a deep breath, one hand clamped around
Cath Kidston secateurs,
and replied: 'Stop making the eyes at me,

I'll stop making the eyes at you.'
He slotted Django on the deck.
The room twisted with gypsy jazz.
Call it a non sequitur.

By jingo, things were getting weirder!
'It's for you.' He lobbed a Nokia,
raised tempo on the turntable.
The phone was flashing *Private Number.*
It was on T-Mobile.
What was that ringtone? I couldn't find a rhythm.
I pressed the green button
and – 'Welcome to South Yorkshire Traveline!' –
I was third in the queue. When she told me
to jump on the eighty or eighty-two
and don't lose a second,
Rolex shot me a balled All Day Saver
with his thumb and trigger finger.

This is how it happened.
The driver barely turned.
Faces cast back rows, boxed eggs. I waded in
and a tide pushed back like gravity.
I felt like a perch in an eddy. My feet
could get no purchase.
Fishing for handrails, I couldn't place my body.
The aisle of the bus stretched on and on
to a vanishing point upstream.
I might have been mistaken
but I thought I heard my name.
The seats were all taken.

Jarvis, thrown by a jolt, groped hand pulls,
riding surf like a capital
C, sans serif.
Smoking heavily, Richard Hawley
shunned the polite notice, his shirt peppered
with baccy curls. White noise
crazed the headset of the drummer
with one arm from Def Leppard.

In tight tees and skinny-legs, the three were black as hags.
The bus rocked. I spotted Rolex
chopping lines on a Metro
with a plastic Maestro. Outside, snack bars
blurred into one cheese melt.
Some kind of runaway bus. I had to get out –

I pressed the button and *Stopping!*
lit up in red, the bus
raced, I pressed and pressed;
the driver turned and grinned.
He was covered in blood.
A wen behind his ear glowed bright blood red.
The sides of the bus fell outwards, the roof
flew clean off to reveal
mirror-deep sky
doubling the clocks and backstreets,
fences, new-build flats, until I lost
what could be real and what reflected.
One stray wheel rolled past and fell flat, spinning;
the tracks
are long finished. The stylus kicks.

André Naffis-Sahley

The Translator
for Michael Hofmann

Unshaven and barefoot, as if on a pilgrimage.
His house is blue: the walls, the carpet, the cups;
the kind of blue you see in sad monasteries,

the paint veined and peeling, with brittle bits of gold
hanging on in the rims. Like Gottfried Benn –
a spiritual father figure – he likes to stay home:

where the coffee is better and there is no small-talk.
He seems scattered, has lost a book somewhere:
a translation. All his life he has hidden a language,

now he eats, breathes and interprets it. Later,
our awkwardness spilled over Hampstead Heath,
where we walked, mostly in silence. We had soup

and beer around the corner, then took a short-cut
to the bus stop, and he was gone; brought by the wind,
taken back by it: the soft-spoken wunderkind of despair.

Cath Nichols

Something Settling

It's like the scum of fat that thickens
on the gravy in the fridge, and when
it was fresh and hot the fat hung
in tiny drops and you didn't mind,
but now you take a spoon and scrape
it off, and wouldn't dream of stirring
it back in again, even though it has
always been there; even though
it was always part of what you poured
on your roast dinner yesterday.
Today it turns your stomach.

Alistair Noon

Conversation with Professor Smirnitsky

Face me across our compartment and feed me
your cold potatoes and pickled eggs.
The landscape's a Tolstoy, best read at speed.
To talk with you is to exercise my legs.

I have used your 55,000 entries
to understand poets, post and prose,
to follow Bulgakov up to the sentence
It was the severed head of Berlioz.

In the exploration of new minerals,
I have used you for The Truth surrounding
the sale of communal flats in Kaliningrad.
As the headwords fly from your mouth,

they dangle a string of chemical phrases,
the atoms adhering into molecules.
Your gold lettering fades and fades,
but the black binding somehow stays glued.

How is the work on the editorial commission
where you pluck double bass in a black quartet
of my two notebooks and Mandelstam's fission
of words, those instruments with no frets?

I think I can hear my language changing,
along the iron framework of the bridge
across the Volga that the team start repainting
before they have even finished.

Andrew Oldham

In the Mist

There is Paris on a distant hill,
a telecommunications mast when all is clear.
A trawler makes its way across the moors,
scuppers oil from it decks
a black ship to sink by the shore.

I unpack the heroes,
boxed and broken in the move.
Scott is gone in a jiffy, looking for Oates
last lost in the land of Shiloh
snow blind, mist blind, biscuited and buggered.

A humpback whale breaks the ridge of pots and pans
dives down with Ahab by his side, frantically texting
so close to the Eiffel tower but no signal
he yells to Ishmael, I have accidentally deleted all my contacts –
Twitter me, twirl me, find me on Ahabandthewhale dot com.

Out now, farther –
Unto the lands of the Houyhnhnms and Gulliver
clutching Swift by the lapel as they ride astride Black Beauty
a thousand Irish clad in babies break out of the heather swords in
        hand.
Singing Bess, Bess, bless her heart and bless her breast.

Scrieving into the long grass Stanley and Livingstone,
lost again, parting ways, taking telephone numbers,
mementos, pocket handkerchiefs, pinkie rings
and parting kisses that linger
arms and lips percussive to the end.

The mist thickens, my phone rings.
A friend from across the valley texts me,
Your house has sails on, limp against the fog waves.
You are floundering against the rocks, I reply
the Marie Celeste can't text at the moment.

Ben Parker

The Way

Drive again through the last outlying
rain-shuttered village, beyond
the final fuel stop, past where the road inclines
inclines again, then levels out.
Tune the radio to the dead melodies
of that country's only great composer
and focus on the dwindling road ahead.
As you move outside the station's reach
wait for the rising background static
to mingle with the trumpet's sombre melody
and when the final note is lost beneath that black scrawl
crank the volume dial clockwise
drop your windows, let your car become
a needle in a groove of infinite diameter.
That sound is not the shifting of the continents,
not the heaving of the gathered clouds
or stretching of the oak's dark roots.
That sound is not your lover's breath
but tonight it's near enough.

Bobby Parker

The Silent Man

Our line drifted in the rolling humps
of green sea below the pier. Dad smoked
a stinking cigarette, indifferent, my moody
monosyllabic hero. The line tightened,
I slowly pulled a twitching crab
into our silent world and up
onto the pier, its pincers rattling on the cement.
We looked at it for a while. The sun
skipped off seawater puddles
and grinned inside my empty bucket.
We didn't know how to pull out the hook.
Dad cursed under his breath and nudged
the stupid crab with one of his holiday shoes.
He lifted it into the air. My mother
watched us from the beach, waving as she took
a photograph of father and son
holding a blurred problem between them.
He tossed the crab into the bucket
along with the line and the orange handle
and when he sighed, I sighed
and when the sky darkened, dad's face
darkened, and when the rain touched my face
he lit another cigarette and started walking.

Sandeep Parmar

June 16, 1956. The Church of St. George the Martyr

It will be fifty years soon.
And yet it seems the preparations have not begun,
for there are still thoughts of winter
in the boughs above Queen Square.

A drake flies overhead. I think he is lost.
His cry is like a man who is to wed.

And what a day it must have been,
the stones of the old church have not forgotten,
though the preparations for your wedding
do not feel as though they have begun.

And yet too late, and so, too late,
the couple that hurries in through the parish gate
welcomes the spirits in empty pews that are to be
their only guests. So, it is the same as it was then.

But it is not the same and yet it is, time will make
much of this and much of you and yet it cannot be the same.

A man, bustles into the square in a black raincoat
like someone in a scare, frightens the cashmere
gentlemen that back away from him
and his immortal packages. In each arm he carries ten
or more Styrofoam boxes labelled 'human organ'
and runs and runs, hoping to arrive before the knowledge
of their death blackens the skins of his beating carriage.

The preparations have arrived and gone.
We hustle the dead around and imagine
somehow that they are alive, that time could still ferry you
back and transplant you untarnished in this beginning.

The sky is late, later than it was fifty years ago that day
when you, having married, were carried out hurriedly
in something pink and knitted with one summer rose,
that blossomed in your hand in Bloomsbury on Bloomsday.

129

Abigail Parry

Craneflies

Late summer, and the long grass is woozy with them,
Staggering on pale threads: the vague, ecstatic kisses
  Of a mad mind flushed to profligate invention.
As though the worried ground gave back our dead
        In frail, fitful hints –
Misguidedly, but with the best intentions.

These are the nightmares dreamed by pampas heads –
The brittle, graphite spoke the sundial strikes
  At noon, the no-sound of the absent bell,
And wristbones braceleted with thread. Too still,
        The catgut stretched too tight,
The gardens thrum. The grasses rave. You know

How the knock-kneed staircase hobbles down to dark –
That marionettes, and hair, and jointed feet
  Of arthropods have stitched the journey down.
And teetering on callipers, they come,
        The pin-legged men, uniquely
Nightmared into being, deeply sown.

Andrew Philip

MacAdam Takes to the Sea

Unhooked from its tenter, the sea drifts off
to arrive at a new understanding
with the earth
                while MacAdam, wearied
and clean out of Red Bull,
                     walks to the edge
of the land he's always called home.

Pure force of habit, that locution:
                    he has come
to feel more at home on the move these days —
on the move and in the dark.

               Aye, but there's dark
and dark the dawn has marvelled at.
It's hidden from him yet, but MacAdam
must drive through such a gloom
to witness how
               lightly the morning rises from its knees.
For now,
        we leave him wading
waist deep into the loosened waves.

Heather Phillipson

Encounter in the New Language

In the washing machine's drum is an odd regatta.
Many days turn into a knot of coloured hosiery
at the termination of a rapid spin cycle.

Bookcases are far from reassuring, my love.
Literature is too exciting, enmeshes you in its concerns
and irregular verbs, half-lost in personal sundry items.

Disengagement from this scene could take some little time.
Tights do not offer assistance, have no authority,
say nothing aloud, and, all in all, tights have it easy.

They languish in a crumpled history of legs and feet,
indifferent to global events and individual responsibility,
like seven proud daughters in an epic of coincidences,

exhilarated from a whirl around the great lake,
not happy because their toes are soaked, not unhappy
because their toes are soaked.

Sophie Playle

Napkin Swans

I wanted to know where the napkin swans came from.
Perched on the tables, waiting to be unfurled. So I stayed
after closing, and from under the folds of red cloth, I saw

the mother swan, a deity worshiped by the touch
of the kitchen boy. Her long white neck stretched
in the candlelight. Her wings spread.

He sang to her in tribal moans, and she stayed silent, her mouth
a black egg, until he untangled himself from her white flesh
and sat folding napkins, watching her sleep.

Her long white body pulsed with breath
as she unfurled.

Clare Pollard

Kingdom

Primroses
for Heshu Yones,

eyebright
for Banaz Mahmod,

feverfew
for Tuley Goren,

selfheal
for Samaira Nazir,

violets
for Asiyah Khan,

lady's bedstraw
for Shafilea Ahmed,

bluebells
for Uzma Rahan.

Simon Pomery

Eulalia

That midsummer week of many marriages,
many flowers thrown over the bright courts
under our feet, what was it we felt
we were made of, getting lost in the city?

Light, air, the greenness of parakeets.
The petals fell
over a maze of lanes, my girlfriend, and the friend
I no longer wish to know,

over two women sharing a needle
as if at a picnic, on cloistered grass
by the Cathedral of Saint Eulalia,
as one of them dropped, flat on her back;

the petals went on falling past the other woman
who smiled as the sun came out of nowhere,
and with the needle still inside her vein
she raised her arms skyward, like a maenad or a saint.

Kate Potts

Un-History

I have studied evacuees, rationing, the Maginot Line, *British Cinema of the 1940s*. I'm young, graduate, able, a cataloguer of behaviour as if an interloper at the zoo. I busy the rememberers with questions, screen-clips of David Niven's pluck, kohl-black fighter-planes stuttering out over the English Channel – a mirroring seam of rucked silver. My falseness, my foolishness, razes to a blush of chaff and dust. The past turns itself up in ironware and sensory ticks, the shallows of faces, their hallows and bones, wellings in breath. It's told how friends and sweethearts met to plan a party and the house was hit. None survived. On Sunday, their wedge of empty pews bowed with an absent mass of haunches, macintoshes, winter boots. The congregation would not see or speak of it. Farther back, in 'the last place on earth God made and

135

forgot to finish' the Jarrow men, washed red-rare, hungry in their Sunday suits, marched off for parliament. Everyone's brother trumpeted in a dance band. Everyone practised the lindy for the church-hall hop, would walk an hour to the office, or factory, or home to stay in darning stockings or sewing a box-pleat, weeding the garden vegetable plot. Sex was first a dicey, incorrigible thing, best performed in the dark or out on the commons, like witchery, and never safe until after the wedding. Those girls, squiffy or mickey-finn'd, who did it with soldiers and swelled, bellies like beanpods, were quietly disappeared.

In all this, there will be one who joined the Eastern fleet
and never saw the bombs hit home, who –
nineteen, from Leytonstone,
a rack-ribbed tug of body – saw Africa and Singapore.

The sea-reflected light made all mass cut-out sharp;
the green of the land was so green he thought it painted on. He
    remembers,
most of all, the flying fish. They'd shoal and hang like scaled spirits,
    fatted dragonflies
kissing the boat's bows. Their falling back pitted the ocean's glass
    like rain.

He saw himself grow backwards to a scorched and stringy boy,
back to the old cheek and nous, the skies shook out, slackening each
    day.
He'd never thought he had the right.

Eileen Pun

Termites in our Tuskawilla House

All we want on a Saturday is one day in our own benign custody.
No, I am not her. She is my mother. If you want, I can get her. No?
I have to go to the patio, through the French doors where outside
feels busier or sweatier, like the whole world is in behind-the-scenes
production. My father has the job to hum like a lawnmower. My
        brother,
to throw an encyclopedia set – one by one – out of a window. Ditch.
Ditch. Ditch. Ditch. I know he's just playing. Bouncing a beach ball
against the stucco. I say, *the mister for the air conditioning is coming.*

She is deep frying, outdoors because the sky doesn't stain. The pan oil
gone thin, hungrily takes each slip of food, foams its mouth, then
        hushes.
I say again, *the mister for the air conditioning is coming.*
My mother's face has become that weary private war of hers
against interlopers of all kinds: swearing, sultriness, swindlers.
She freshens her floured hand against her skirt. Her body is a clean
island, sometimes she even goes to church by herself. My older sister,
not at home is free to come and go. On the telephone, people can't tell
the three of us apart. I go back inside where me and the overhead fan
are alone together, swooning.

When the mister arrives, he goes right up to the side door.
The lawnmower coughs and stops, like someone motioned at the
        throat
'cut it off'. By default, the encyclopedias now seem bigger or falling
from further up. Itch. Itch. Itch. Itch. My father makes all of the usual
        offerings
Iced tea, lemonade, soda with ice? In a minute my mother
is going to tell my brother to quit it, or else. Not another book drops.
As if on cue they come inside, my parents and a man with a wrung out
face, used to giving warnings. It was as if he came to say:
The house is vanishing. Don't be lonely in a family.

137

I don't know why, but I have followed them into the garage.
I stand in-between my parents like an only child. We watch him go
to the air conditioner's portal frame. Rivets come out like it's a stick up.
His face wrings out news. *It's not a problem with your filter. See these?*
Soon my father and the mister are on their knees, tearing out
a clump of the wall like it's a barrage. All over – inside – is a colony,
and I am seized by some good stupidity, overtaken by insult,
the house rapidly changing its own conversation. I wonder,
where is my brother? *Termites.* Says the mister.
You'll have to fumigate those suckers.

On a Saturday, we just want that cooked all day supper,
and we curl around the meal like five sisterly fingers.
While my mother is saying grace, I think I can hear them
satisfying themselves, mindless and breeding – horrible
in the huge pleasure of their eating. If only they could be still
for a moment, at the same time, like we are now, indivisible –
we would never want to kill anything that could be stilled.

Rufo Quintavalle

Names and the animals

Some poets know the names
of almost all the animals
and what they do
is they deploy them
not all at once
but a smattering
to bring the animals
into focus
and make them
enter their poems

but all I hear
is man, is me
and it isn't the animals
come but language;

the tug of barbed
wire or an abattoir's
heavy plastic
flap is where
the animals rub
against our world
like strangers
in the tube
like messengers
not names.

Edward Ragg

Some Other Mea Culpa

That the wind-wards wise of blame
Is a cloak or curtain drape in which

A certain child folds the pleats, I know;
That, walking, if I angle my wrists

Neither can you clasp the world in a ball
Nor find yourself flying, as if we could

Do nothing but flying... That I have
Worried about the figures of balances

And less the balance of figures is
A seminal crime and, worse still,

Understandable, that it is understandable.
To have clasped, then understood the

Innumerable un-understandable things
At first light is, likewise, a crime,

If worth committing, that, also in the
Written line they have understood it

Or find it understandable, that this too is
A kind of crime I should have committed.

Vidyan Ravinthiran

A chair addresses Jackie Chan

As you somersault into my seat and spin
my legs in a henchman's face, I know
I love you, always have... Though one
might consider ours an abusive relationship.
Your own bruises, do they remember
how I held you, moved just as you desired
– or am I simply more of the scenery
bullets chewed to make that crucial
Inch haruwwin my epintaping loon
and yours enthralling as the Gaza Strip
played for laughs? You are the realist
and I am a piece of your code, the mundane
detail which makes this room appear
an actual room in which to live and fight
to keep well-wrought urns from tottering
off their improbably thin pedestals,
holding before your face the explosive vest
so the gun-toting tough is comically arrested.
Yet I know my worth. I know you
have nightmares, of empty rooms, with no
urns or kitchen sinks or silly little chairs
to work with. There, your kung-fu bricolage
shrivels to nothing like the limbs of a saint.

Toby Martinez de la Rivas

from **Terror**

Gehenna

My uttermost music will be whining or ágonal gasping,
unadorned plainchant of approximants, barely stressed.
Do not tell this, but I come awake at times, the burning
rick in my head, the flayed tarpaulin risen in vehement
admixtures of wheat and plastic, plus several panicked
cut-outs lumbering through mown stalks backlit by fire
cursing down phones, or holding still with lit cigarettes
in formal postures of despair: bereft, as those that slept
the hour, hair luminously thinned, shabbily bejacketed.
In the spoilt marches of his night, keep your watch late.

Tenement

The little tract of the body I work over, as in the vision
of Arcimboldo reified by Methodius of the Bonwetsch
edition: thistle in the heart, the raptuorous, dead eyelid
an ear of wheat, scarified palea, sweetgrass at the nape
of the neck tickling the skull-base, heaped strawberries
and heaped cherries, the allotment in summer awaiting
its dissolution. Soon stormclouds will come dispensing
benedictions from the black horizon, ash leaves scatter
the tilth of glass fragments and jagged laths: otherwise
kempt tenement of ire, of *yea*, of plausible resurrection.

Darkly

Immanent, blindly vested in the shapes of its restraint,
fire here transformed into sheets of rainwater sheaves
off gutters, gleams of shadowed light implicit in each
transparent, folding curtain: inward, borne, sustaining.
Drumming of hoisted umbrellas, a sudden bright river
of wind driving the black sparks of a flock of starlings
to the belltower, clouds encased in outward substance
ridden as sexual bodies, fond tenements of indwelling,
lux tenebrae, the word at once disclosed and withheld.
Append this, I beseech you, to your *Syllabus of Errors*.

Chasse

In that sense, I am less a facsimile than a simulacrum
of myself unfallen, made in that image, razored Book
of Hours face-up in fragments of windowglass: *scène
de chasse* as primary illustration, the searing emerald
of the oak, squealing boarlets, dogs snapping at a doe
half sunk in flowers, huntsmen *en fête* lifting clarions
to the stilled havoc of air: say January, the sun falling
beneath a superimposed zodiac, larks snagged in nets
weeping, venting that famous tongue: the tongue that
is so gently spoken at times, so pathetically adequate.

Blackdowns

To narrate is to relent: in me there sháll bé no relenting,
storm baiting the fields with light, the deathless instant
of outhouses, cars prone on gravel in reeking greyscale,
the copse hard by the storage tank deepening its covert.
Who steps with me into the shadows, allegiant, sudden,
if not yóu, from the foothills out across the bare Levels,
the briefest image regnant even at the point of collapse.
Nów turquoise lightning thrústs among the stark ridges,
the water discloses in a moment the shape of its tresses,
cropped birches are lashed, stoop, immaculate with fire.

desolate

Testament

Look, it is March as it always ís, the disordered spectra
rainbowed in wet asphalt or élse invisible, hi-vis power
walkers buried in music jerking their heads defensively
in time, pitbulls barely tethered, the clotted buds of ash
groping to-usward, salvation's blind or suffering intent.
Also in time: the supernumerary rainbows stanchioned
in glassy shallows overflying both Huish and Langport
re-assert their covenant: áre, wére, overbearingly bright
signals of conviction, promissory against black nimbus.
As Neruda's *violeta*, self-collapsing. In *corolla of rage*

Sam Riviere

Poem

When I'm feeling unsure or upset
I get drunk and give myself a haircut
after midnight in poor light
with the smallest mirror I can come by
because the decisions I make
when cutting my hair are the same
as the decisions I make in my life or writing
only quicker snip snip snip I hardly think
just keep going till it looks about even
and I find myself pulling a long lock
from the crown or over the ear
and I don't want to cut it
so long as it's there the job isn't done
but I know I might not see
its like again in this life
and that's how I find the weak spot
in my mind something like a stain or a storm
on the heart a cloud that comes over
whiting one eye because
in the run of this hour
one long strand of hair
doesn't have any right or reason to be here
doesn't make any sense but
I am not going to cut it I am not
going to cut it just yet

Declan Ryan

Et In Arcadia Ego

You are beside me on my sofa
shoes off
feet up

Our hands are Coventry Cathedral
in the ruins
of my lap

Jacob Sam-La Rose

Rapture

From the headlines of *The New York Times*
front page, James Barron reports it's judgement day
tomorrow. I'm jogging, headphones in my ears,
Friday morning in the local park and I don't feel

prepared. There's sunlight in the spaces between
the leaves, and all the other things I haven't seen
or done, but of course, none of that matters
now. I've lost track of the judgement days

incoming. My money was on 2012, the ancient
Mayan calendar. The ice shelves are falling,
our mobile phones confuse the bees,
and the mushroom clouds that overshadowed

my youth still wait offstage to do their dirty work.
Who was it that said that everyone's an atheist
until the plane goes down? Last night, a woman crossed
my path at the top of a flight of stairs and asked

if I was superstitious. I never knew that was bad luck,
but even the things you don't believe in can get you
at the end. There's the man who built a clock
in a desert, underground, designed to keep perfect time

for 10,000 years, and there's a mountain stuffed with
nuclear waste that requires a warning sign with an expiration
date pitched far beyond any languages we currently know.
And rapture, which I always believed was the sound you made

with someone's tongue at work against a private stretch
of skin, the way some part of you is carried away.
I don't know if I've done enough to make the roll-call
of the celestial spaceship some would say is coming

for them. I'd like to believe the park I'm jogging round
will still be here tomorrow, with the dogs still nosing
at each other's flanks, oblivious. Jogging, which is itself
a form of prayer for an unknown future, all that moving

forward step by step. Tonight, says the man who built
the clock, the hour and minute hand will pass
the midnight mark and no one knows
how many times they've done that before.

The next song in my ears carries the line
come get me, 'cause we don't have much time left.
Perhaps our truer days of rapture or judgement
are less grand, or much more local, while

elsewhere, the world still turns.

Anna Selby

Drowning Before The Silt

She's drowning as her toe
tips her into the river.
She's held her breath three years passed ten
and it is too late to stop the watch
that keeps reminding her
it is not morning,
it is not evening,
then if only lunch
could lurch her lurhop off the desh
and dash her round a tree.
Then the ball of her foot sinks deeper.
She doesn't hold the sides,
doesn't even reach out
like you bob up a bloated hand
before a meeting.
She shakes off her rings.
Watches them sink.
And she is drowning before the silt
slides her skirt up her thighs.
She is tired of kicking away from edges.
All is still in her mouth.
There are no more corners.
She had drowned before she met the stream.
The river, the river was nothing but encouragement.

Colette Sensier

We'll meet again

My grandfather believed
in total resurrection of the body,
he'd watch my fingernails
drop into the washbasin,

into my father's mouth
when I was a baby, later,
into the depths of carpet
underneath my bed.

Each time he cut my hair
a little bit more of my mortality
slipped down my back into the world.
No need for organs to stay put,

they were free to fly
out of my broken skin
(replenishable with pints
of spilled blood hanging in bags

at the cosmic butchers.)
My liver, kidneys, heart
could be called back like dogs –
he didn't doubt his original hip

would come running at the final call,
that last light, when his family
would gather round his bed,
when a life's worth of fingernails

would follow his slipstream
up to Heaven, to coat him
like feathers on an Aztec eagle
as he sat at God's intact right hand.

Owen Sheers

Harvest
i.m. Elizabeth Roberts

I picked early apples the day I came to see you,
slow-stepping round each low crown
to reach an upturned palm and twist each apple once –
unscrewing bulbs from the tree's chandelier.

Some gave themselves easily,
while others remained stubborn on the branch,
their stems cording but holding,
as at my feet the windfalls performed

their annual trick, a Trojan-Horse illusion
only to reveal, with a nudge of my boot,
the cavities of their wasp-eaten insides.

I carried the good ones back in the sling of my jumper,
so later, when I reached for your hand,
an apple leaf fell to the sheet.
In a poem such as this, that leaf might turn

your knuckles into the growth scars of twigs,
while seeing your face so sunken, without teeth,
might conjure up those wasps again. But this wasn't a poem,
this was you, still holding, your memories rising

to bring the Highlands and the veldt to your afternoon bed,
so all I saw instead was that recollection in your eye,
sharp enough to fool myself this wasn't,
after all, the last goodbye.

One week later and your daughter called.
A single twist, she said, somewhere between midnight
and dawn, and you were gone.
As I replaced the phone my eye cast the room

only to find, and this I swear is true, those apples again,
still crowding their bowl, and above them an afternoon wasp,
its scribbled search for fresher air
writing this last line across the window pane.

149

Kathryn Simmonds

Oversleeping

And there are the clothes you dropped, the arms of a green shirt
raised in surrender, the slough of nylon
and a dress of apricot wool.
Sit up and see the sheets fine wired with pubic hair and eyelashes,
skin cells scattered like flakes of pre-history.

Your clothes have been going out of fashion,
quickly like the turning of a pear, slowly like a bone bleaching. No
      matter,
pick up the leather boots you loved so much,
zip them right up to the knee and walk;
you are Jairus's daughter, passing through
the convalescent house, its shelves of misremembered books,
its shivers of dust.

What else is there to do but open windows, let the outside tumble in
like washing from a glorious machine. See
the day is half over, but still blue. Step out and balance
on the ledge. Below a brown bird darts
over the garages, another yanks a worm from its clay bed
and flies with it – fly worm, fly!

Your leg hair stands to gold attention. Courage now, step out,
feel the plummet, then the catch and
you're up, swimming in cold, eyes streaming.

There is the park where you broke your wrist, there is the church
where you first met God and the playground of children
whose children are running through cities now, as the river
runs, a silver speck, coursing

underneath the disappearing viaduct, running through the valley
      passing
fields where horses gather, trapped in their nature.
The houses reposition themselves
and there are your arms, the arms
that used to be useless, parting pale belts of cloud.

Anna Smaill

After Reading Wallace Stevens

I dream and enter a green place,
a place I imagine to be called Claude, Montana.

There are no other people
(the green of a past of several hundred years),

but my mother is there
and we are pleased to see each other.

We make a start on naming things.
The animals we sort in pairs.

We begin with salamander.

V. A. Sola Smith

Sylvia

You were a panzer, horrifyingly
technical in your approach,
thin armoured, yet a panzerkampfwagen

no less. You bit off two wars,
one famously; you pocked its cheek
with your fire. You knew how to kiss

and you were hungry, more,
ravenous. Your artillery swelled.
With the insatiable promise of life's loss,

you became awesome. More, now
your death drive was astounding.
My wheels get stuck. I find myself

stopped in your tracks, immobilised,
a useless model death machine of your design.
Once, I too was a glad victim. Of the men you killed,

I feel too. Only, *I* cannot say I do.
Ich, I cannot kill, nor be. Your ghost
tyre marks tyrannizing page after page.

Martha Sprackland

Leaving the Road

At the turnoff to Boadilla del Monte your car
touches the embankment,
the gentlest meeting of wheel and earth which
sends the car upwards.

Your eyes are in the rearview mirror,
one hand on the wheel,
the other leaving my thigh like a bird, launched
into sudden flight.

Inside the car there are only fractions.
Your foot at the pedal takes years
my fingers reaching for you slow
to milliseconds
and I remember, fleetingly,
the lit sign over the motorway which
you helped me translate.
A 150 no se salva nadie.

Remember when my mother visited?
She sat in the back seat as we sped her
along the vast strip of the M80.
I felt so adult, that day
in my city, with my lover, singing songs in Spanish,
my mother the child strapped into the backseat
not understanding any of the words.
I was cavalier about the speeding,
about the *pipas* and fag ends littering the bar floors
the leering men, the reek of piss on Calle la Palma.

You're swearing. The seconds mount, endless
and we're suspended in the air
one tyre blown, the others hanging
redundant. Your breath covers me, cariño
chicle and cigarettes.

Imagine the landing, the jolt
and the clout of machinery.

Or, if you prefer, imagine this –
The ritual lighting of my cigarette from his,
the engine silenced for the ascent,
the land slipping away, undeserving.

Camellia Stafford

Navigation

I ask the thoughts, the words to say them: come back to me.
It is a way to look. To see the curlicues in the design of the frame
while absorbed in the narrative of the painting,
able to sense the room behind oneself,
the people within it, to know some of their preoccupations
not through guesswork but with assurance.

I have found myself lost in the practical,
in learning to think of how to be okay after noticing life.
Mine revealed to me not as a day by day carnival
nor I as the lead in a set of thrillingly ill constructed scenes
but as the undernourished pulse of an aimless vessel,
whose sails grow tatty with dreaming.

This is melodramatic. I almost resent its irresistibility.
Now I have asked, the words come back to me,
they grow out of themselves, become perhaps not what I want
to say but scurry over the page like a swarm of ants
who carry their dead back close to the nest. A journey
must end and it did with a damaged bookcase,

a floral eyesore of a lamp, loved for its out there-ness,
numerous other possessions but they are just things,
the things I can't bring myself to part with. I have a newish mind
which has its own new thoughts. Old tricksters drop in
from time to time to vie with my rationale. I have memories.
I mean I can have them without excruciating nostalgia.

Here is one:
I am sitting in the bedroom of my old flat in Camden.
It is 4am-ish.
I have just finished writing a poem.
I shall give it to my friend at the airport tomorrow.
I have fallen in love with him.
He is returning to Australia.
The sky is tourmaline.
I think of him flying through it.

Ben Stainton

Once more, Jack

In the orange corner they dance
like pinpricks, delivery laced
with   inexpensive   champagne.
Tony, overplaying his urbane
murderer, drags a line along
the scuff of E's knee: 'I saved
some of the red stuff in a ginger
beer bottle.' Our Lapsed Hermit
throws up in the felt inglenook.
Like a chair-lift I ease forward,
furtive; abrupt. Their words are
corseted, misspelt idiots.   She
affects naïve under the glare
of my halogen probe.   From
the bottom of a glass I dolly
across her lips, trying to acquire
the eye between blasé & RAGE
while our foreign director litters
the set with nerves. 'How brutal
should things get?' 'Pretty brutal...
beatific.' They touch like two
fingers rammed in a socket, one
hand unleashing the other. I
frame the mutilated bodies well.

Elizabeth Stefanidi

In doubt

In doubt sir
Take me for a ride
Now I know why people like to travel

In doubt sir
In despair madam
Theatres on my mind, chaos

In doubt sir
Cause I want to go to bed early
And wake up late

In doubt sir
Please let me sleep here
In your bed

With your life
In doubt sir
Because I have nothing else to do

Jon Stone

Mimic Octopus

You aquanaut, you fifteen-things-in-one,
you even have the seabed bamboozled,
not knowing when to rest and when to churn
and churn into a turbid underworld!
I see each supple arm's in on the plan
and all are, by the crimelord nerve-sprawl, willed
into a sudden fish, a venom-keen
nest of quills, a rack of claw, or spooled
beneath your ocarina heart, then strewn –
your rubber heart's own flexible scaffold
now so much snake. So call you estuarine
or almost water, half crossed the threshold
into creature. Now a quoit, a spear,
now black as the bunraku puppeteer.

Chloe Stopa-Hunt

The Raspberry-Eater

Surreptitious in the canes I was discovered, little fruit
splitting – such culpable and brute pink gems.

Lay by the bare canes after; listened to
the codes of the breeze blowing their dry way through.

Brown apples weighed the grass, which had slashed my legs halfway
to the knees with stripes. It was a fine busy botanical day

for going to seek my fortune undisgraced – I packed a jar
of nubbed ginger, carried (luck's yellow kisses) a stolen pyrite star.

Agnieszka Studzinska

Emergency

I hold her between hip and breastbone
watch the tidy outpouring of water from a running tap
break as I slit the current with a glass & then she stiffens,
flops to one side & shakes, eyes rolling back
as if all the sunlight she has known has entered her body
& won't let go. I clutch her with all the water left in mine,
run down the hallway, opening the door
calling her name as if she was running too fast in front of me,
ignoring the things I had not yet managed to tell her &
the neighbour's gate is too stiff and I push & push,
yelling so hard that the veins on my face break like a web
tearing the threads between us – I heard someone say,
get her to theatre, keep pushing. How I pushed for you then
in your resistance to enter – wild kicking
like that of my foot on the gate, the word *ambulance*
stitching the air & my neighbour in the background
& you somewhere watching us all, crouching on the floor
as if we were looking for something that we couldn't
recover or claim as our own, not ever – not truly –
I thought how fragile an afternoon always is,
your body slowing as the sun clipped us all
& the paramedics saying *she's o.k.*
as the hurtle of crying brought you back
unlike the first time, when you entered silently,
an odour of snow on my skin.

Kelley Swain

Questions of Travel
after Bishop

Let me shed these smothering albatrosses
as I cross the Atlantic.

Let me moult these heavinesses
from my neck as I wing west.
The greatest furies can astonish; bring peace
in the smallest gesture: as palm to palm

is holy palmers' kiss. Give me your hand, then,
and bring me calm as you bring me storms

which sweep me from my founderings.
I'm learning all the ways to drown.

Tiffany Anne Tondut

Way of a Wanton

Everybody
wants you
buxom, brazen
burning
as you slip
into yards
of yellow rape.
Zephyrs fan you
pollen snuff,
gods deliver you
scents, then
faint. Madame
your boudoir
crawls with
suits who strip
drip, beg
for thunder.
Rabbits dust
your cheeks
with fur, shit
you strings
of soft brown
pearls. I burn
for you, your
deadly wick.
You give me
fever, a rash
I want to lick.

Claire Trévien

Rusty Sea

The tide creaked to a halt on Tuesday. Fishermen's boats
sailed to its end and watched the drop (twenty metres).
Wednesday, children walked to the wall: threw ropes,
pitched their hands like hooks to rouse the weavers.
Men lay ladders against the salty-hedge and dived.

Saturday, the sea turned brown, shutters clattered
closed to keep the stink out. Dead fish burst the surface,
seagulls flew so far in they forgot to return. Weeds clambered
up, tentacles piercing the plane, midges drew laced
patterns in the sky. We waited for the tide to start again.

Broken stones, boned sand, and wrinkled mud hurried
their layering. The sea solidified as outside, the rocks rolled
in. Boulders, smoothed from the trip but pierced by a hole,
so that they seemed like an army of eyeballs, boldly
gathered by the wall of sea that had turned to rust.

Simon Turner

Brummagem Jazz

What a feeling, to step out of the musty
twilight bookshop air with a collection
of poetry under your arm & run smack
into a bleach-blonde brassy bellow of a day:
clear blue sky like a sheet of tarpaulin,
no clouds, & blossom on every visible tree.
This dirty old city's never looked so spruce.
Even the Sally Army band look jazzed up
in their threads, hugging their silver trombones,
but not as jazzed up as the man in black
(& I really mean black: a black overcoat
running all the way down to his knees,
black boots, black shades, & strangler's gloves)
striding up the street with a sax to his lips,
blowing his soul out into the air, blossom
cascading off the trees in crazy fistfuls
in a sudden wind which can only have sprung
from the gaping mouth of his instrument.
I mean, it's like he's the master & maker
of the city itself: the wheeling gulls, the crowds,
the fountains, the monuments, the bus-stops,
all of it nothing but a figment of his music,
the silence waiting at the end of his song
wide & absolute as a record's run-off groove.

Jack Underwood

Gottlieb

If I leave you here you will surely die,
as sure as the worms will find your pockets.

I'll carry you beyond that ridge.
Which is more than reasonable.
You are a heavy man and I have my own
skin to lift. Leave behind your letters
to your puppy kids and rabbit wife,
I cannot risk the extra weight.

In the morning you may be found.
Your eyes will be filled with water, daylight
and the yellow beaks of gulls.

Ryan Van Winkle

The Ocean I Call Mine

Flies land on her wrist, legs, the tips of her eyes
remind us we are alive. 'Go find something dead,'
she says. And the sun is here for us, the wind
takes our hair like a sail. The ocean I call mine
as if I was floating inside its womb. She says
she feels this too. We are looking at the stretch
of our mother –
both of us from the same place, but opposite. And
it is strange to look at an ocean you've known
your whole life and to see it from another side.
Like catching
your mother drinking a beer before church on Sunday.
You must look at her and admit Yes – this is my mother.
Flies will land on the lip of her glass. Gentle as a tide
she will brush them away. One shore is not a woman
nor a man. You need a boat to see them in their swell.
And I wonder if I am anything like an ocean or
if I can surprise someone by opening my hand as a wave.
May I too have a moment in sunlight when a boy or a girl
will look at me and say, 'Father,
Father I need a boat.'

Todd Von Joel

Company

When I got ripped out, forceps, C sec; on my own.
When him then Mickey left, I was left; on my own.
When I found love, lost love, first time; on my own.
When I'd tried everything by fourteen; on my own.
When I went from a boy to a lout to a man; on my own.

When I got expelled, kicked out, moved in; on my own.
When I lost the plot that time, permanent marker smile; on my own.
When you all ducked out, I was still swinging; on my own.
When I went down, rode bird, came back galvanised; on my own.
When I found that thing in Bimbo's thing, I was all broken; on my
    own.

When I wanted more, bigger better things; on my own.
When I done the Access, big step back then forwards; on my own.
When her scheme flopped, not sectioned, fuck you; on my own.
When I started Kingston, class full of people; on my own.
When I cleaned the blood off, moved out quickly, lucky boy; on my
    own.

When I wake up, turn kiss Spinny; on my own.
When I went Gran's funeral, own pew, own thoughts; on my own.
When I pray, say sorry, think back what I've done – belly ache; on my
    own.
When I'm winning in the ring, undefeated, knocked him out first
    round; on my own.
When the black dog bites, 3 month cycle, ready for you; on my own.

When I stop drinking, I'll stop drinking; on my own.
When I pass, done well, graduation; on my own.
When I make it, if I ever make it, really wanna make it; on my own.
When he dies, big drink, no remorse, steady lip; on my own.
When I see the bright light, dark tunnel, march on, not scared; on my
    own.

Ahren Warner

Μνημοσύνη

The smackhead's hands are soft and clammy
like the just-lathered palms of my mother.
I remember

his pupils are an absolute
torpor, a squall of fear, and have me
as a little boy in the doorway, watching

my mother in the midst of laundry
and tears, and what seemed inconceivable
grief.

It is the give of his skin that lingers
or muscles its way back in, *here*

between that Cranach the Elder crucifixion
and this crucifixion by an elderly Cranach.

Rachel Warrington

To catch a swan

After midsummer when, primaries shed,
they are flightless, close the birds in a pen:

on the first day, drive them slowly ahead
with boats; on the second have a chain of men
beat through the shallows and finish the chase.

To catch a swan, take the neck with one hand;
with the other, the joint of the left leg. Embrace
the swan, wings to your breast, upright. Stand.

You can also take an apprentice. She
has to be close to learn, and is then
vulnerable:
        tell her, keep her wrists free
of the claws and do not imagine
a god took this form in order to rape
with ease. Watch for the wings; hold him by the nape.

Tom Weir

The Outsider

As I climb onto the gate my foot slips on the wet steel.
I cling on with my arms, my body, and vault over;
the wet ground moves beneath my feet as I land.

It's not raining but the air's damp, moisture clings to it like
        condensation to glass.
There's a sheep caught on a barbed wire fence at the edge of the field,
but by the time I get to it the knotted steel blades have snagged

its coat like fish-hooks. You're beside it, trying to spook
it back onto the path but you can't, you just drive it further back.
I try to help you but its coat is thick and wound so tight

I cannot get a good grip. It's frightened; I can feel its muscles
quivering somewhere beneath all the wool. You move me out the way
and try to yank it free. The sound of the sheep's wool

tearing is like cloth. It cries as if you've torn its skin
then bolts, suddenly, like a greyhound released from its trap.
I go after it, try to guide it back into the field

but it's too quick, finds its own way, leaves clouds of its frantic breath
turning on the air; wisps of its torn coat,
still covered in mud and shit, stringing from the wire fence.

Anne Welsh

My Major Retrospective
after Tracey Emin

I try to tell you my life till now:
                    monochrome punctuated
by pink neon squiggles; lanes that led nowhere but coupling,
once; the ships on the Clyde that formed a Halloween mask
at dusk with the windows of the building behind them.
                                      You
try to describe the sea at Margate, though I've never been,
so it quickly becomes my native Ayrshire coastline, mixed
with that white candyfloss transience I smelt once at Brighton,
the day I knew I would leave my husband.
                                We talk of books,
you think of cheap editions, pregnant with woodpulp;
I'm cloth and horseglue, bound tight and tooled in buckram.

It seems we'll never find a common tongue, then suddenly rudbeckia,
sunshine yellow that you say makes you think of me:
pierced in the core by cones brown and hard like mahogany.
They're familiar and familial: not quite my mother's marguerites –
                    darker, stronger, more robust somehow,
                      though who could survive more than my mother?

Later, walking the back route home, we count the fireflies in the dark
and speak only in passing pub signs and the names of local breweries.

Through each Black Horse and Royal Oak you name,
I think of you with all those past women, speculate
their legs were thinner, breasts more pert, stomachs
certainly flatter,
                like what matter to you are random pieces of flesh

not the atoms that form strings tumbling from mouth to page,
the magnetic letters you leave waiting on my fridge
that don't quite spell I love you yet,
                          the bedroom window
                          open to the gardenfall below.

Sarah Westcott

Alien

I arrive at night, touch down
on your counterpane, feet-first,
like Mary Poppins.
All I have with me are the clothes
I was born in, two silver studs
punched into each lobe, a swallow
tattoo, my tongue.

I move among you, feeling
halogen, mistral, gorse-scratch, longing,
my new hair lifting and tangling
under the eiderdown.
The first shit is a revelation,
the insistence of plaque shows me how you live.
I learn to pack my bag with Pringles,
toothpicks, the Lord's Prayer.

Only when I'm swimming
in enormous liquid afternoons
can I escape the circadian,
look beyond the sky.
For years I move beneath strip lighting
an angel hiding in the nettles
and none of you need ever know.

Lizzie Whyman

Meteorology

Mother always said I had the weather in me.
When it raged I could slice Newton's tree in half.

I am not proud that last night as we ditched the group
I shrugged off my smile, quick as chiffon

at the kerbside where you pissed. My face
was faster than a sky-shift, cooler than the moon's.

I should have said then, *Forgive me, I am full of forces
I cannot name,* but the sky cracked open,

electricity seeking release, burning memory, a caustic
fizz as sparks tried to catch on air between us.

Every car was a tornado heading for home.
To me the laws of physics don't come easy

but under these unweaving skies I've no need for a key
or a kite to bring me down to earth:

you can hold a whole weather system in your arms,
tell it to breathe and, later, treat the burns.

Ben Wilkinson

Open Return

Whatever brings us back to step off the second-to-last
train having shuttled down the West Coast mainline
here we go again: automatic doors open onto hail;
Victoria Park yawns; three or four pigeons dart
across laughing at those caught brolly-less in T-shirts.
A taxi pulls up. We clamber in, set off through silver-
streaked streets, half expecting to spot familiar faces
as the weather tunes down to sleet. But while the place
is the same, to us it's still changed – each landmark,
shop and side-alley pub a facsimile of its former self,
menaced by our memories of them; imaginings
no more real than streets in our driver's satnav system.
On Queensway, a dog tied to railings looks on pitifully:
we pay, climb out and hurry on; my thoughts stuck with
that sail-less windmill which for years has sat redundant.
In the market square, the town hall's motionless clock.
Time flicking the Vs at us, having long since strutted off.

Chrissy Williams

On Getting Boney M's Cover of 'Mary's Boy Child' by Harry Belafonte Stuck in my Head

I bump into a friend in the British Museum
and we try to distract her son, Fin, with plaques
but he wants authentic plastic rainsticks,
white chocolate mummies,
Peter Rabbit in hieroglyphics,
the days of the week in Mayan honey.

Finlay has a poem:

> 'I found a treasure.
> I measured the treasure.
> It was only a centimetre long.'

I shake the six-year-old's hand,
commenting on his chainmail vest,
gold crown and Jedi lightsabre.
I learn that he was born on a Tuesday
and admire his complete lack of pretention.

> He sings paper scarabs
> He sings Parthenon bookmarks
> He sings Centurion pyjamas
> He sings Harry Belafonte
> We sing rubber duck sphinxes
> We sing pencil elephants
> We sing İznik coffeemugs
> We sing Rosetta Stone jigsaws

And how unaccountable the difference
between volume and worth. And how fast
the heart can fill with treasure.

We make things new to make them new.
This is what we do.

Tony Williams

A New Metal

For years now the scientists have been promising us every morning a new miracle,
a new element, a new metal —The Goncourt Journal

Its atomic number is pi, symbol
two Scrabble tiles randomly selected.
Its full name is of course unspeakable and contains
one each of each of the vowels, oxidised so they require
umlauts as ballast and the fifth c a cedilla as anchor.

Dropped in alcohol, it becomes tensile,
or perhaps less so, and may be stamped with guilds'
crowns, shields, mythical beasts and fleurs-de-lys
to show that everything under the sun,
helicopters choking in the desert, flumps,
Silvio Berlusconi and the theme tune of *Cheers*,
existed already, dispersed, in the medieval world.

There are machines that stamp it into cogs
to work the time machines that take us back
to build machines... and so on. You have your fillings done
and eat in other languages. Verbs cast in this metal
may be used as nouns, thingifies usaged as doings,
order words of data strings musical disregarded
generally and buggered with about syntax. Lovely. Dirigible.

It is sentient, and mewls like a cat. Struck with a gong,
it resonates at a frequency audible only to the dead.
This gate is made of it. Step through.

Heidi Williamson

Slide rule

The universe is running away with itself
like a child on a red bike on Christmas Day.

Somewhere the wrapping is still being opened.
The present gives itself again and again.

And the child hurtles at perfect speed
across town towards nothing.

Her parents are already
looking at the clock, saying

how late it is getting, how the darkness
comes so much sooner.

It is only a matter of time,
they are saying,

before she will land,
awkwardly, in an original position,

sucking in broken concrete
and teeth.

Meanwhile,
the child on a red bike

is running away with herself
like the universe on Christmas Day.

Alice Willington

Iconostasis

The way up Belukha is the glacier,
its rocks lifted and turned
into uneven scarps. It seeps
at its terminus into untouchable Eden,
a lake of jade.
We hammered steel into snow
and ice, as if carving out
a dream of mountaineers
in one night's sleep.

                    Dislodged,
it fell away, until the walls
of the tent were a curtain
before the planets, the arched icons.
I dreamed the sun, the moon
and Jupiter eclipsed,
each one of us isolated and split.
In unbearable brightness
I climbed the cathedral.

Jennifer Wong

Glimpse

Brown bread rises
from the toaster.
Time gargles
in a coffee machine.
On the table there's jam,
still sweet, and a soft block of butter.
We stir in milk, then sugar.
This is just one morning.
Outside, a few leaves fall.
There are not many clouds
to be seen, and the day is not that cold,
even a little sunny. Next door
our neighbour unchains his bike,
and you turn to me and say,
'I'll be coming back early.'
We kiss.
This is simple.
And this is one morning.

Luke Wright

Loughborough

I once spent the day with a girl who was pro fox-hunting;
who asked what was wrong with the Tories;
who said she wanted her parents' life.

We lay down outside a church,
the grass poured around us like mint sauce,
and I thought maybe I'd just marry her
and be done with it.

Later, we climbed high to where the Victorian prison stood,
its windows like diamonds in the low sun,
the skyline beneath us like smashed meringue,
and I thought about the house we would own
in Loughborough,
our lanky children,
our utility room,
our dogs, wax jackets, fridge calendar and committees.

We sat on our coats, finger-tips touching,
an ice-cream van started like a chesty cough.
The breeze almost gone, the mud almost dry –
it was all just like summer, if you squinted.

Jane Yeh

The Robots

They meet in secret in electrified rooms.
They are under surveillance... by themselves.
They sneak food out of our kitchens, even though they don't eat it.
The password for the meetings is 'Please admit me, I am a robot' (in
    robot language).

They like to interface with ceramic-coated transistors for recreation.
They keep robo-dwarf hamsters as pets.
They have a financial interest in the Arena Football League, Amway,
    and Red Lobster.
Howsoever you find them, they will appear ready to serve.

If a robot crosses your path, it means your grandmother just died.
In robot language, 'I' and 'you' are the same thing.
How many robots does it take to build a suspension bridge over the
    Grand Canyon?
If you see a robot with its hands folded, it's planning something.

They use our grammar to mock us.
Cicero once wrote, *Roboti non possunt fundi* ('It is not possible to defeat
    the robots').
If they smile at you, it means you just died.
The city of robots will be concentric, well-polished, and paradisiacal —
    for the robots.

In the city of robots, they will celebrate the holidays Bolting and
    Zincfest.
Their love of rabbits will come to the fore.
The rest of us will be snuffed out like vermin.
Happy will the robots be when they can practice kung-fu in the open.

Biographies

Paul Adrian was born in Leeds in 1984, and still lives there. His poem 'Robin in Flight' took First Prize in the 2010 National Poetry Competition.

Rowyda Amin's poems have appeared in magazines including *Magma* and *Wasafiri* and the anthology *Ten* (Bloodaxe, 2010).

Claire Askew is the author of a pamphlet collection, *The Mermaid and the Sailors* (Red Squirrel, 2011), and teaches at Edinburgh's Telford College and the University of Edinburgh.

Tiffany Atkinson was born in 1972 and now lives and works in Aberystwyth. Her first collection *Kink and Particle* (Seren, 2006) was winner of the Jerwood Aldeburgh First Collection Prize, and her second, *Catulla et al* (Bloodaxe 2011), was nominated for the London Poetry prize 2012.

Jay Bernard is from London and currently lives as a resident writer, workshop leader, zinester and traveller in South East Asia. She is a Foyle Young Poets alumnus and her first pamphlet is entitled *Your Sign is Cuckoo, Girl* (Tall-Lighthouse, 2008).

Giuseppe Bartoli was born in 1983 in Virginia. He has lived in Peru, Chile, Italy, France, Scotland, Spain, Argentina and England.

Emily Berry's debut full-length collection of poems will be published by Faber & Faber in 2013.

Liz Berry was born in 1980 in the Black Country and now lives in London where she works as an infant school teacher. Her debut pamphlet is *The Patron Saint of Schoolgirls* (Tall-Lighthouse, 2010).

Caroline Bird won an Eric Gregory Award in 2002. Her third collection, *Watering Can*, was published November 2009 and achieved a Poetry Book Society Recommendation.

Julia Bird grew up in Gloucestershire and now lives in London. *Hannah and the Monk*, her first collection, was published by Salt in 2008, and a second collection is due in 2012.

Rachael Boast was born in Suffolk in 1975. *Sidereal* (2011) won the Forward Felix Dennis Prize for Best First Collection, and was also short-listed for the Aldeburgh First Collection Prize and long-listed for the *Guardian* First Book Award.

Jemma Borg was born in Essex in 1970. She read zoology at Oxford and has a doctorate in genetics. In 2007 she won the New Writing Ventures Award for Poetry.

Siddhartha Bose is a poet, playwright, actor and a Leverhulme Fellow in Drama at the University of London. His first collection is *Kalagora* (Penned in the Margins, 2010)

Laura Bottomley was born in 1985 in Shrewsbury, Shropshire. She has an MFA in Creative Writing from Kingston University.

Penny Boxall was born in 1987 in Surrey. She graduated in 2009 from the University of East Anglia with an MA in Creative Writing (Poetry). Her poetry has appeared in *The Salt Book of Younger Poets*.

David Briggs was born in Hampshire in 1972. He received an Eric Gregory Award in 2002, and his first full collection, *The Method Men* (Salt, 2010), was shortlisted for the London Festival New Poetry Award.

Zoë Brigley, PhD, was born in 1981 and grew up in Wales, but now lives in America. Her first collection, *The Secret* (Bloodaxe, 2007), was a Poetry Book Society Recommendation. *Conquest* (Bloodaxe), is out in 2012.

Phil Brown was born in Surrey in 1987. In 2009 he was shortlisted for the Crashaw Prize and won the Eric Gregory Award in 2010. His debut collection is *Il Avilit* (Nine Arches Press, 2011).

Mark Burnhope was born in 1982. He studied at London School of Theology before completing an MA in Creative Writing at Brunel University. He is in *The Best British Poetry 2011* (Salt).

Jenna Butler, PhD, was born in Norwich in 1980. Her collection, *Aphelion*, appeared with NeWest Press (Canada) in 2010, and *Songs for a Broken Season* and *Wells*, are forthcoming in 2012.

James Byrne's second collection is *Blood/Sugar* (Arc, 2009). For ten years he has edited *The Wolf*. He is the co-editor of *Voice Recognition: 21 Poets for the 21ˢᵗ Century*. He is poet in residence at Clare Hall, Cambridge.

Christian Campbell's first book, *Running the Dusk* (Peepal Tree Press, 2010), won the 2010 Aldeburgh First Collection Prize (UK) and was a finalist for the Forward Prize for Best First Collection.

Niall Campbell, from the island of South Uist, studied English Literature at Glasgow University. In 2011 he received an Eric Gregory Award from the Society of Authors.

Vahni Capildeo, PhD, was born in Trinidad in 1973. *Dark & Unaccustomed Words* (Egg Box Publishing) followed *No Traveller Returns* (Salt, 2003), *Person Animal Figure* (Landfill, 2005) and *Undraining Sea.*

Melanie Challenger was born in Oxford in 1977 and now lives in the Scottish Highlands. She is the author of one collection of poems, *Galatea* (Salt, 2006), and a winner of an Eric Gregory Award.

John Challis was born in Essex in 1984. In 2010 he was awarded AHRC funding to study for an MA in Creative Writing at Newcastle University.

John Clegg was born in 1986 and grew up in Cambridge. He lives in Durham, where he is studying for a PhD. A full collection, *Antler*, is forthcoming from Salt in 2012.

Ross Cogan was born in Kent in 1970, and studied philosophy, gaining a PhD from Bristol University. In 1999, he received an Eric Gregory Award. His first collection is *Stalin's Desk* (Oversteps, 2005).

Jane Commane was born in Coventry in 1983 and is co-editor of Nine Arches Press and *Under the Radar*. She has worked as a writing tutor in a variety of settings. Her poems have been included in *The Best British Poetry 2011* (Salt Publishing, 2011).

Swithun Cooper has had poems published in *Magma, Poetry London, The Rialto* and *The North*. He won an Eric Gregory Award in 2009.

Sarah Corbett grew up in North Wales and lives in Yorkshire. Her collections are *The Red Wardrobe*, 1998, shortlisted for a Forward First Collection and the T.S. Eliot prize, *The Witch Bag*, 2002, and *Other Beasts*, 2008 (all published by Seren).

Emily Critchley has a PhD in contemporary American women's experimental writing and philosophy from the University of Cambridge, where she was the recipient of the John Kinsella and Tracy Ryan Poetry Prize in 2004. Her Selected Writing, *Love / All That / & OK* was published by Penned in the Margins in 2011.

Abi Curtis was born in 1976. She won an Eric Gregory Award in 2004. Her first collection, *Unexpected Weather* (2009), was a recipient of Salt Publishing's Crashaw Prize. She has a PhD in Creative and Critical Writing from the University of Sussex.

Rishi Dastidar was born in 1977 and now lives in London. He was a runner-up in the 2011 Cardiff International Poetry Competition.

Amy De'Ath was born in Suffolk. Her poems have appeared the *Salt Book of Younger Poets* (2011) and *Best British Poetry* (Salt, 2011). Her first collection, *Erec & Enide*, was published by Salt in 2011.

Antony Dunn has published three collections of poems: *Pilots and Navigators* (Oxford Poets, 1998), *Flying Fish* (Carcanet Oxford Poets, 2002) and *Bugs* (Carcanet Oxford Poets, 2009).

Joe Dunthorne was born in Swansea. His debut novel, *Submarine*, was translated in to ten languages and made into a film. His debut poetry pamphlet was published by Faber & Faber. His second novel is *Wild Abandon*.

Rhian Edwards' first collection of poems is *Clueless Dogs* (Seren, 2012). Her pamphlet, *Parade the Fib* (Tall-Lighthouse, 2008), was awarded the Poetry Book Society pamphlet choice for autumn 2008.

Michael Egan was born in Liverpool in 1980. His first collection is *Steak & Stations* (Penned in the Margins, 2010). He has recently been Highly Commended by the Forward Prize.

Inua Ellams was born in Nigeria. His poems appear in anthologies: *City State* (Penned in the Margins, 2009) and *The Salt Book of Younger Poets* (Salt, 2011).

Lamorna Elmer was born in Devon in 1988. Her work has been published in the anthology, *This Line is not for Turning: the Anthology of Contemporary British Prose Poetry* (Cinnamon).

Andrew Fentham was born in Birmingham in 1986. His work has appeared in magazines including *Poetry Review*, *Brand*, *The London Magazine*, and *The Rialto*.

S.J. Fowler is the author of four full collections of poetry, the latest being *Minimum Security Prison Dentistry* (AAA press) and the *Lamb Pit* (Eggbox).

Alexander Freer was born in Stockport in 1989. He has recently graduated from a BA in English literature from the University of Warwick, where he edited *Angelic Dynamo* magazine with John Clegg.

Isabel Galleymore was born in Camberwell, London in 1988. She has a BA in English Literature from The University of Reading, 2010.

Alan Gillis was born in Belfast in 1973. He is Lecturer in English at The University of Edinburgh. His poetry books are *Somebody, Somewhere* (2004), *Hawks and Doves* (2007), and *Here Comes the Night* (2010), published by The Gallery Press. He has been shortlisted for the T.S. Eliot Prize.

James Goodman was born in 1972 in Canterbury, Kent, and grew up in Cornwall. His poems have appeared in various magazines and his first published collection of poems is *Claytown* (Salt Publishing, 2011).

Kélina Gotman, PhD, is a Lecturer in Theatre and Performance Studies in the Department of English Language and Literature at King's College London.

Kathryn Gray was born in Wales in 1973. She received an Eric Gregory Award in 2001. Her first collection, *The Never-Never* (Seren), was shortlisted for the T.S. Eliot Prize and the Forward Prize for Best First Collection.

Matthew Gregory was born in Suffolk, England, in 1984. His poems have appeared in *The Best British Poetry 2011*, the anthology series *Stop Sharpening Your Knives*, and have been aired on BBC radio. In 2010, he received an Eric Gregory award.

Neil Gregory was born in Surrey in 1981 and now lives in Wimbledon. He is currently studying for a BA in English Literature and Creative Writing at Kingston University.

Jen Hadfield was born in Cheshire in 1978 and lives in Shetland. Her second collection, *Nigh-No-Place*, the second of her two collections published by Bloodaxe, won the T S Eliot prize in 2008.

Nathan Hamilton is a poet and publisher. He runs Egg Box Publishing and is chairman of the board of directors for Inpress. He is editing the Bloodaxe anthology *Dear World and Everyone In It: New Poetry in the UK*.

Sophie Hannah is a best-selling crime writer of international repute, as well as a widely-published poet. Her fifth poetry collection, *Pessimism for Beginners*, was shortlisted for the 2007 T.S. Eliot Prize.

A.F. Harrold is an English poet working for both adults and children, on the page and on the stage. He has had a number of collections published.

Oli Hazzard was born in Bristol in 1986. His poems have appeared in various anthologies including *The Salt Book of Younger Poets*, *New Poetries V* (Carcanet) and *Best British Poetry 2011*; his first collection, *Between Two Windows*, is from Carcanet (2012).

Lindsey Holland was born in south Lancashire in 1976 and has an MA in Writing from the University of Warwick. Her pamphlet, *Particle Soup,* will be published by Holdfire Press in early 2012.

Matthew Hollis was born in Norwich in 1971. *Ground Water* (Bloodaxe, 2004) was shortlisted for the Guardian First Book Award, the Whitbread Prize and the Forward Prize for Best First Collection. *Now All Roads to France: the Last Years of Edward Thomas* (Faber, 2011) won a Costa prize in 2012.

Wayne Holloway-Smith was born in Wiltshire in 1979. His debut pamphlet, *Beloved, in case you've been wondering*, was published by Donut Press in 2011.

Holly Hopkins was born in 1982 in Ascot. She studied Literature at the University of Warwick and now lives in London. She received an Eric Gregory Award in 2011.

Adam Horovitz was born in London in 1971 and raised in Slad, Gloucestershire. His debut collection, *Turning*, was published by Headland in 2011.

Martin Jackson was born in Warrington in 1981. His poetry won an Eric Gregory Award in 2011.

Samantha Jackson has a first class degree in English Literature from the University of East Anglia and has just completed an MA in Creative and Life Writing at Goldsmiths, University of London.

Heidi James, PhD, was born in Kent in 1973. She was a columnist for *Dazed and Confused*, and her work has been featured in various magazines, journals and anthologies.

Sarah James is a Worcestershire journalist, fiction writer and poet. Her first full-length poetry collection is *Into the Yell* (Circaidy Gregory Press).

Andrew Jamison was born in Co. Down in 1986. His debut pamphlet, *The Bus from Belfast*, won the 2011 Templar Poetry Prize.

Anna Johnson is a founder member of the Forest Poets, based in North London. She is published in four other anthologies of new British Writing.

Evan Jones was born in Toronto, Canada, and has lived in Manchester since 2005. His first collection is *Nothing Fell Today But Rain* (Fitzhenry & Whiteside, 2003). His second is *Paralogues* (Carcanet, 2012).

Francesca Jones was born in Bristol in 1989 and grew up on the South Coast of England. She has recently completed an MA in Creative Writing and Publishing at Kingston University.

Joshua Jones recently graduated from the University of East Anglia and is due to start an MA at Sussex. His poetry and criticism has appeared in a variety of venues, including *The Rialto*'s U35s feature. *A Kind of Awe* (2011) is published by Red Ceilings, and his debut collection, *Thought Disorder* (2010), is by Knives Forks and Spoons.

Meirion Jordan was born in South Wales, near Swansea. He studied mathematics at Oxford, where he won the Newdigate Prize. His first collection of poetry, *Moonrise*, was shortlisted for the Forward Prize for Best First Collection.

Michael Kavanagh has lived in England and Scotland for over ten years. His poetry for children has been published in the anthologies *Read Me At School* (MacMillan), and *Michael Rosen's A-Z, The Best Children's Poetry From Agard to Zephaniah* (Puffin).

Luke Kennard, PhD, was born in 1981. He has published many collections of poetry with Salt, including *The Solex Brothers*, *The Harbour Beyond the Movie* (shortlisted for the Forward Prize for Best Collection in 2007) and *The Migraine Hotel*.

Amy Key was born in Dover in 1978 and grew up in Kent and the North East. Her pamphlet is *Instead of Stars* (Tall-Lighthouse, 2009).

Katharine Kilalea's first book, *One Eye'd Leigh* (from Carcanet) was shortlisted for the 2009 Costa Poetry Awards.

Simon King was born and raised in Grimsby. He holds a Masters with Distinction in Creative Writing from Kingston University.

Caleb Klaces was born in Birmingham in 1983. His chapbook is *All Safe All Well* (Flarestack Poets, 2011).

Richard Lambert was born in London in 1971, and has a PhD in medieval history. His pamphlet *The Magnolia* was published by Rialto in 2008.

Agnes Lehoczky was born in Budapest in 1976. She holds a PhD in Critical and Creative Writing from the University of East Anglia. Her collections, *Budapest to Babel*, (2008) and *Rememberer* (2011) were published by Egg Box.

Frances Leviston was born in Edinburgh in 1982 and grew up in Sheffield. Her first collection, *Public Dream*, was published by Picador in 2007 and shortlisted for the T.S. Eliot Prize, and the Forward Prize for Best First Collection.

Joanne Limburg was born in London in 1970. Her first collection, *Femenismo* (Bloodaxe) was shortlisted for the Forward Best First Collection Prize. Her second, *Paraphernalia* (Bloodaxe, 2007) was a PBS Recommendation.

Fran Lock's debut collection, *Flatrock*, was published by Little Episodes in 2011.

Kim Lockwood was born in Yorkshire in 1988. A poem of hers appears in the Everyman's Library Anthology, *Villanelles* (2012). She is co-editor of this anthology.

Mike Loveday has an MA in Creative Writing from Kingston University. He is editor-publisher of *14* magazine.

Hannah Lowe was born in Ilford, Essex in 1976. She studied American Literature at the University of Sussex and has an MA in Refugee Studies.

Alex MacDonald was born in Essex in 1986 and studied English at Goldsmiths College, London, and currently lives and works in London.

Sophie Mackintosh was born in South Wales in 1988, and recently graduated with a degree in English and Creative Writing from the University of Warwick.

Lorraine Mariner was born in Essex in 1974. She works at the Poetry Library, and lives in London. Her collection, *Furniture*, was published by Picador in 2009 and shortlisted for the Forward Prize for Best First Collection.

Kathryn Maris was born in New York in 1971. Her first poetry collection, *The Book of Jobs*, was published in 2006, and her second will appear from Seren in 2013. She lives in London.

Toby Martinez de las Rivas was born in 1978. He received an Eric Gregory award in 2005 and had a pamphlet published as part of the Faber New Poets series in 2009.

Sophie Mayer, PhD, was born in Middlesex in 1978. She was awarded an Eric Gregory in 2004. Her full collections are *Her Various Scalpels* (Shearsman, 2009) and *The Private Parts of Girls* (Salt, 2011).

Chris McCabe was born in Liverpool in 1977 and works in London at the Poetry Library. His first collection, *The Hutton Inquiry*, was published by Salt in 2005 and was followed by *Zeppelins* in 2008. His latest book, *The Restructure*, has just been published by Salt.

Richie McCaffery, born 1986, has poems in *Agenda, Stand, The Rialto, Iota, Envoi* and many other magazines and e-zines.

John McCullough was born in Watford in 1978. His collection, *The Frost Fairs*, was published by Salt in 2011.

Michelle McGrane lives in Johannesburg. Her collection, *The Suitable Girl* (2011), is published by Pinddrop Press in the United Kingdom and Modjaji Books in South Africa.

Michael McKimm was born in Belfast in 1983. The author of *Still This Need* (Heaventree Press, 2009), he won an Eric Gregory Award in 2007.

Alex McRae was born in London in 1979 and now lives in America. She studied English at Pembroke College, Oxford. She won an Eric Gregory Award in 2009.

Isabella Mead was born in 1983 in Cambridge. She holds a Master's Degree in History of Art, specialising in Modernist Sculpture.

Emily Middleton was born in Bristol in 1990, and grew up in Derbyshire. She has recently finished a degree in Philosophy, Politics and Economics at Oxford University. She was a winner of the Foyle Young Poets Award in 2005 and 2006.

James Midgley was born in Windsor in 1986. He holds an MA with distinction from the University of East Anglia. In 2008 he received an Eric Gregory award.

Stefan Mohamed was born in Kingston-Upon-Thames in 1988, but has spent most of his life in Wales. He returned to Kingston to study Creative Writing. In December 2010 he won the inaugural Sony Reader Award, a new category of the Dylan Thomas Prize, for his debut novel *Bitter Sixteen*.

Kim Moore is originally from Leicester. She now lives in Barrow in Furness in Cumbria and works as a brass teacher. In 2011 she won an Eric Gregory Award and the Geoffrey Dearmer Prize.

Helen Mort was born in Sheffield in 1985. She received an Eric Gregory Award from The Society of Authors in 2007 and won the Manchester Young Writer Prize in 2008. Her first collection is forthcoming from Chatto & Windus in 2013.

Beverley Nadin was born in Swindon in 1981. She has an MA in Creative Writing from Sheffield Hallam University. She won the 2009 Poetry Business Pamphlet Competition Sheffield Prize and is working towards a PhD in Creative Writing at Newcastle University.

André Naffis-Sahely was born in 1985. His translations of Abdellatif Laâbi's *The Bottom of the Jar* (Archipelago Books) and Rachid Boudjedra's *The Barbary Figs* (Arabia Books) will be published later this year.

Cath Nichols, PhD, was born in 1970 and grew up in Papua New Guinea, New Zealand and Britain (Kent). She lives in the north-west of England and has had poetry and plays produced for radio and stage.

Alistair Noon was born in 1970 and lives in Berlin. His poetry and translations from German and Russian have appeared in nine chapbooks from small presses. *Earth Records*, his first full-length collection, is from Nine Arches Press (2012).

Andrew Oldham was born in Bolton in 1975. His first collection, *Ghosts of a Low Moon* (Lapwing, Belfast), was published in 2010.

Ben Parker was born in Worcester in 1982. In 2008 he completed a creative writing MA at the University of East Anglia. He now lives in Oxford.

Bobby Parker was born in Kidderminster in 1982. His published books include *Ghost Town Music* (The Knives Forks and Spoons Press) and *Digging for Toys* (Indigo Dreams Publishing).

Sandeep Parmar, PhD, was born in Nottingham in 1979 and raised in Southern California. She edited the Collected Poems of the modernist poet Hope Mirrlees for Carcanet Press (2011). Her debut collection, *The Marble Orchard*, was published by Shearsman in 2012.

Abigail Parry was born in Aldershot in 1983. She has been published in *The Best British Poetry 2011* from Salt, and in 2010 received an Eric Gregory Award.

Andrew Philip was born in Aberdeen in 1975. His first collection, *The Ambulance Box*, (Salt Publishing, 2009), was shortlisted for the Aldeburgh First Collection Prize, the Scottish Arts Council First Book Award and the Seamus Heaney Centre Prize.

Heather Phillipson was born in London in 1978. She received an Eric Gregory Award in 2008. Her pamphlet is published by Faber & Faber.

Sophie Playle was born in 1987 and has lived most of her life in Essex and Hertfordshire. She is on the Creative Writing MA at Royal Holloway.

Clare Pollard was born in Bolton in 1978 and now lives in East London. Her first collection, *The Heavy-Petting Zoo*, (Bloodaxe, 1998) received an Eric Gregory Award, and her most recent, *Changeling* (Bloodaxe, 2011) is a Poetry Book Society Recommendation. She recently co-edited the Bloodaxe anthology *Voice Recognition: 21 Poets for the 21st Century*.

Simon Pomery was born in Galway in 1982 to an Irish mother and English father. A pamphlet of Pomery's work, *The Stream*, was published by Tall-Lighthouse in 2010.

Kate Potts was born in 1978 and grew up in London. Her work features in the Bloodaxe anthology *Voice Recognition*, in Salt's *Best British Poetry 2011* and in *The Forward Book of poetry 2012*. Her collection *Pure Hustle* was published by Bloodaxe in 2011.

Eileen Pun was born in New York. She now lives in Grasmere, Cumbria. In 2011 Eileen was selected as an Escalator prize-winner by Writers' Centre Norwich and also awarded a writing and research grant by Arts Council England.

Rufo Quintavalle was born in London in 1978, and now lives in Paris. He is the author of three books, including *Dog, cock, ape and viper* (corrupt press, 2011) and *Liquiddity* (Oystercatcher Press, 2011).

Edward Ragg was born in 1976 in Stockton-on-Tees and now lives in Beijing. He is an Associate Professor at Tsinghua University and has published two books on the work of Wallace Stevens.

Vidyan Ravinthiran is a research fellow at Selwyn College, Cambridge. His poems have been anthologised in *Joining Music With Reason* (Waywiser Press, 2010), *The Salt Book of Younger Poets* (Salt, 2011) and *The Best British Poetry* (Salt, 2011).

Sam Riviere co-edits the anthology series *Stop Sharpening Your Knives*, and received a 2009 Eric Gregory Award. His debut collection is from Faber & Faber later in in 2012.

Declan Ryan was born in Mayo, Ireland. He has an MA in Creative Writing from Royal Holloway and organises and hosts the London poetry event, *Days of Roses.*

Jacob Sam-La Rose is a London-based poet, freelance artistic director for literature in education initiatives and poetry editor for flipped eye publishing. His first full collection, *Breaking Silence*, was published by Bloodaxe in 2011.

Anna Selby was born in Shropshire in 1982. She is a graduate of the Creative Writing MA at the University of East Anglia. Anna works as Literature and Spoken Word Co-ordinator at the Southbank Centre.

Colette Sensier is a writer from Brighton. She studied English at Cambridge. She has been a first-prize winner of the Foyle's, Peterloo and Tower young people's poetry prizes, and featured in the anthologies *Best British Poetry 2011* and *The Salt Book of Younger Poets*.

Owen Sheers is the author of two poetry collections, *The Blue Book* (short-listed for the Welsh Book of the Year and the Forward Prize Best First Collection) and *Skirrid Hill* (winner of the Somerset Maugham Award). Owen's first novel, *Resistance*, was made into a film.

Kathryn Simmonds was born in Hertfordshire in 1972. She won an Eric Gregory Award in 2002. Her collection *Sunday at the Skin Launderette* won the Forward Prize for best first collection in 2008 and was short listed for the Costa Poetry Award.

Anna Smaill was born in New Zealand. She holds a PhD in English Literature from University College London. Her first collection of poetry, *The Violinist in Spring*, was published in 2005 by Victoria University Press.

V.A. Sola Smith was born 1988, in Lancashire, England. She took an MA in Contemporary Prose Fiction, at Kingston, graduating with Distinction in 2010.

Martha Sprackland was born in Barnstaple in 1988. She is twice-winner of the Foyle Young Poets of the Year Award and editor of *Cake* magazine.

Camellia Stafford has an MA in Contemporary British Art from the Courtauld Institute of Art. Her debut pamphlet, *another pretty colour, another break for air* is from Tall-Lighthouse (2007).

Ben Stainton was born in 1978. A first collection, *The Jealousies*, was published in 2008 and an experimental pamphlet, *The Backlists*, in 2011.

Elizabeth Stefanidi was born in Liverpool in 1980 and holds both a Greek and English passport. She has studied Media and Cultural Studies at the London College of Printing.

Jon Stone is a co-editor of Sidekick Books and *Fuselit* magazine. A full collection, *School of Forgery* (Salt, 2012), is imminent.

Chloe Stopa-Hunt attended New College, Oxford, where she took a double first in English and was awarded the English Poem on a Sacred Subject Prize 2010. She has twice been a Foyle Young Poet of the Year.

Agnieszka Studzinska was born in Poland in 1975. She has an MA in Creative Writing from the University of East Anglia. *Snow Calling*, her debut from Salt, was shortlisted for the London Festival New Poetry Award 2010.

Kelley Swain was born in Rhode Island and moved to London in 2007. In 2009, her first collection, *Darwin's Microscope*, was published by Flambard. Kelley is Writer-in-Residence at the Whipple Museum of the History of Science, Cambridge.

Todd Swift, PhD, is Lecturer in Creative Writing at The Kingston Writing School, Kingston University. He is the author of eight collections of poetry, including *Seaway: New & Selected Poems* (Salmon Publishing, 2008). He has been Oxfam's poet-in-residence since 2004 running their renowned reading series in Marylebone.

Tiffany Anne Tondut was born in Cambridge, 1981. She has been writing and performing prize-winning poetry since childhood. She has an MA in Creative Writing from Kingston University.

Claire Trévien was born in 1985 in Brittany. Her first poetry pamphlet *,Low-Tide Lottery* is published by Salt, and her next collection is due in 2013 with Penned in the Margins. She is the editor of *Sabotage Reviews*.

Simon Turner was born in Birmingham in 1980. His first collection, *You Are Here*, appeared in 2007. Nine Arches Press published *Difficult Second Album* in 2010.

Jack Underwood was born in Norwich in 1984. He has a PhD in Creative Writing from Goldsmiths College, where he teaches. He won an Eric Gregory Award in 2007 and was named a Faber New Poet in 2009.

Ryan Van Winkle was born in New Haven in 1977. His first collection *Tomorrow, We Will Live Here* was published by Salt in 2009. He lives in Edinburgh.

Todd Von Joel was born in south London in 1982. In 2010 he graduated with a First Class BA Honours degree in Creative Writing and Drama from Kingston University.

Ahren Warner grew up in Lincolnshire. His first collection, *Conifer*, (Bloodaxe 2011), was a Poetry Book Society Recommendation and was shortlisted for the Forward Prize for Best First Collection.

Rachel Warrington was born in Dorset. She has a BA in English from Cambridge, and was commended in the 2002 Bridport Prize poetry competition.

Tom Weir was born in Guisborough in 1980. He holds an MA in Creative Writing from Bath Spa University.

Anne Welsh was born in Scotland in 1972. She is a Lecturer at University College London, where she is completing a PhD on the poetry and short stories of Walter de la Mare.

Sarah Westcott was born in Oxford in 1974, grew up in Devon and lives in London where she works as a reporter for the *Daily Express*. She has been commended in the inaugural South Bank Poetry competition.

Lizzie Whyman's poetry has been widely published in magazines and anthologies. In 2006 she won the Poetry Can national poetry competition and was runner up in the Cinnamon Press competition.

Ben Wilkinson was born in Stafford, Staffordshire in 1985. He was awarded an MA in Writing from Sheffield Hallam University. He was shortlisted for the inaugural Picador Poetry Prize.

Chrissy Williams has been published in the anthologies *Best British Poetry 2011* (Salt) and *Stop / Sharpening / Your / Knives* (Egg Box). A pamphlet, *The Jam Trap* (Soaring Penguin), was published in early 2012.

Tony Williams was born in Derbyshire, in 1977. His first collection, *The Corner of Arundel Lane and Charles Street* (Salt, 2009), was shortlisted for the Aldeburgh, Portico and Michael Murphy Prizes.

Heidi Williamson is currently poet-in-residence at the John Jarrold Printing Museum in Norwich. Her first collection, *Electric Shadow,* (Bloodaxe Books, 2011) was a Poetry Book Society Recommendation.

Alice Willington was born in Perthshire in 1974. 'Iconostasis' (originally entitled 'Prelude') was awarded Second Prize in the Ledbury Poetry Competition in 2009.

Jennifer Wong was born in Hong Kong in 1978. She won a scholarship to study English at Oxford and took an MA in creative writing at the University of East Anglia. She has a forthcoming poetry collection with Salmon Poetry.

Luke Wright was born in London in 1982. He has two books published by Nasty Little Press. He appears regularly on BBC radio. He lives in Suffolk with his wife and son.

Jane Yeh's collection, *Marabou,* was published by Carcanet and shortlisted for the Whitbread, Forward, and Jerwood Aldeburgh prizes. Her second collection is *The Ninjas* (Carcanet, 2012).